Everyday Embellishments

8 FUN QUILTS TO STITCH AND EMBELLISH

M'Liss Rae Hawley

Martingale®
& COMPANY

CREDITS

President: *Nancy J. Martin*
CEO: *Daniel J. Martin*
Publisher: *Jane Hamada*
Editorial Director: *Mary V. Green*
Managing Editor: *Tina Cook*
Technical Editor: *Laurie Baker*
Copy Editor: *Karen Koll*
Design Director: *Stan Green*
Illustrator: *Laurel Strand*
Cover and Text Designer: *Trina Stahl*
Photographer: *Brent Kane*

MISSION STATEMENT

*Dedicated to providing quality products
and service to inspire creativity.*

Everyday Embellishments: 8 Fun Quilts to Stitch and Embellish
© 2003 by M'Liss Rae Hawley

That Patchwork Place®
is an imprint of Martingale & Company®.

Martingale & Company
20205 144th Avenue NE
Woodinville, WA 98072-8478
www.martingale-pub.com

Printed in China
08 07 06 05 04 03   8 7 6 5 4 3 2 1

Library of Congress Cataloging-in-Publication Data
Hawley, M'Liss Rae.
    Everyday embellishments : 8 fun quilts to stitch and embellish / M'Liss Rae Hawley.
        p. cm.
    ISBN 1-56477-479-1
  1. Patchwork—Patterns. 2. Quilting—Patterns.
  3. Patchwork quilts. I. Title.
    TT835.H3485 2003
    746.46'041—dc21
                                              2002156269

Dedication

To my fabulous husband, Michael A. Hawley, sheriff of Island County, bestselling mystery writer, and great dad. Thank you for ironing my fabrics for the past twenty-five years.

To our son, Corporal Alexander Walsh Hawley, United States Marine Corps. Parents could not be more proud of a son than we are of you. Wherever you are in the world, *Semper Fi!*

To our daughter, Adrienne Blythe Hawley, scholar, golf champion, first French horn, great baker, chef, and all-around wonderful person. The best to you as you embark on your college career.

Acknowledgments

I am most grateful and appreciative for the following people and companies that have so generously given their time and products to this book.

Mary V. Green, Editorial Director; Terry Martin, Editorial Assistant; and the entire staff at Martingale & Company

Laurie Baker, technical editor extraordinaire. This book is truly a testament to your skill and patience. We managed to put this book together between ballet, piano lessons, vacations, surgeries, college visits, and on-the-road teaching. Thank you.

Husqvarna Viking, especially Sue Hausmann, Senior Vice President of Education and Consumer Motivation; Tony Kowal, Embroidery Design Specialist; Theresa Robinson, Notions Marketing Specialist; and Nancy Jewell, Publicity Director

Clothworks' owner, David Peha; and Nancy Mahoney, creative consultant

Sulky of America, with special thanks to Patti J. Lee, Vice President of Consumer Relations

Quilters Dream Batting and owner Kathy Thompson

American & Efird, Inc., exclusive importers to the United States of Mettler threads, and Marci Brier, Director of Marketing

Robison-Anton Textiles and Andreea Sparhawk, Product Manager

Vicki DeGraaf and Peggy Johnson, my two "best friends." Thank you for always being available at the last minute to help me meet my deadlines.

Dr. Timothy D. O'Connor and Dr. Paul T. McBride, the two best doctors. Thanks for keeping me going!

Contents

Introduction

AS A DESIGNER and teacher, I am always looking for topics to inspire my students, but this book was actually inspired *because of* my students. For some time now, I have had to deal with critical and chronic illnesses, and it is not always easy for me to travel to teach. During one of the more difficult periods, a loyal following of quilters in my area committed to coming to my home for classes. These quilters are always a source of strength for me, so I wanted them to feel welcome. Nothing is more welcoming than a quilt, so I designed a wall hanging to hang on the inside of my double front door. It would be the last thing they saw as they left and hopefully convey my gratefulness to them, as well as offer inspiration for their own quilt projects.

That was how it all began. Not wanting them to see the same quilt each time they were at my home, I began thinking of more designs that would be appropriate for a door-size space. Knowing that I would probably teach these patterns at some point, I wanted to include a multitude of techniques, both traditional and nontraditional. They had to be fun and they needed to have a unified theme. Designing patterns with a seasonal or holiday theme seemed a natural, and including a variety of embellishment techniques would make each one unique, interesting, and individual. A series was born!

embellish \im-'bel-ish\ . . .
1: to make beautiful with ornamentation: DECORATE
2: to heighten the attractiveness of by adding ornamental details: ENHANCE . . .

Merriam-Webster's
Collegiate Dictionary, Tenth Edition

The quilts in this book are meant to be fun, and as the title implies, a big part of that fun is embellishing them. All of the embellishing techniques are easy enough for the beginner to master, and complete instructions for each technique are given in "Embellishment Basics," beginning on page 10. This section also details a variety of supplies that make the embellishment process easier or faster. Be as generous as you like with the embellishments or add fewer if that is your preference. Use the same type of embellishments as I have, or use whatever you have in your stash that looks interesting. The embellishments are meant to add interest, texture, and fun, and what you add and the quantity you add are strictly up to you.

For each project you will also find a "Design Details" box. Be sure to read the information in the box before purchasing your supplies or cutting the fabrics as you will find everything from tips on the best fabric choice to a cutting shortcut.

I hope you enjoy piecing and embellishing this collection of seasonal wall hangings as much as I have enjoyed designing them. Now go and have fun!

General Instructions

IN THIS SECTION, I will cover some general information that you will find handy for selecting fabrics and for cutting out and stitching together the pieces required to make the projects. All of the supplies and techniques dealing with embellishing will be covered in "Embellishment Basics" beginning on page 10.

Selecting Fabrics

This book is all about embellishing, and for the quilts presented here, you need to think of fabric as part of the process. Normally I would advise that you use only 100%-cotton fabrics, but these quilts have some nontraditional characteristics to them and you can deviate from that traditional advice and use just about any fabric. If it enhances the quilt, then use it! I used everything from upholstery fabric to pieces of my sister-in-law's prom dress to make these quilts.

Of course, the fabrics you use will dictate

> A well-thought-out design, attractive color scheme, and skillful execution will attract a viewer's eye and hold her attention. The details—the embellishments—will draw the viewer in for a closer look and bring her back for more.
>
> *Larkin Van Horn*
> *Award-winning mixed-media*
> *textile artist*

how you will care for the quilt once it is finished. If you want to be able to machine wash your quilt, use fabrics that can endure the process, and prewash any fabrics that you can before beginning the quilt. In "Cinco de Mayo," I used pieces of velvet, taffeta, and silk that will not allow it to be machine washed if cleaning is ever necessary. However, because most of the quilts were designed to be wall hangings, an occasional vacuuming to remove dust will probably suffice. Be sure to also consider the embellishments and any other products that were used in the quilt before cleaning it. Some ribbons and trims, as well as some adhesives, cannot withstand washing or dry cleaning.

Yardage requirements are provided for all of the projects in this book and are based on 42" of usable fabric after preshrinking. For quilts that call for scraps of fabric, you may want to consult the cutting instructions to see how large a piece you will need.

Rotary Cutting

Instructions for quick-and-easy rotary cutting are provided whenever possible; some quilts will also require templates to be used for cutting pieces (refer to "Making Templates" on page 9). For those unfamiliar with rotary cutting, brief guidelines are provided here.

To rotary cut, you will need a rotary cutter, a self-healing mat, and acrylic rulers. The rotary cutter makes quick work of cutting strips, squares, and rectangles. The mat protects the cutter blade and the tabletop. Rulers measure fabric and guide the rotary cutter. There are many sizes available, but I would recommend purchasing at least a 6" x 24" ruler and another square ruler.

All rotary-cutting measurements include ¼" seam allowances.

1. Fold the fabric in half lengthwise, matching the selvages. Place the fabric on the cutting mat with the folded edge closest to you. Align a square ruler, such as a Bias Square®, along the folded edge of the fabric. Butt up a long, straight ruler to the left edge of the square ruler, just covering the uneven raw edges along the left side of the fabric, as shown.

    Remove the square ruler and cut along the right edge of the long ruler. Discard the cut strip. (Reverse this entire procedure if you are left-handed.)

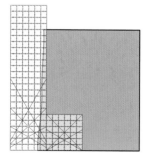 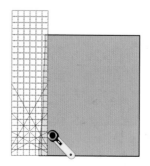

2. Measuring from the straightened edge, cut strips the required width. For example, to cut a 3"-wide strip, align the 3" ruler marking with the edge of the fabric.

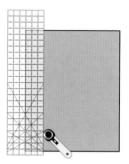

3. Turn each strip horizontally and trim the selvage ends. Cut each strip into pieces of the desired size.

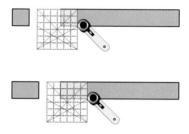

Machine Piecing

Maintaining a consistent ¼" seam allowance is important when you are machine piecing. If you are not consistent, it will affect how the rest of the pieces that make up the quilt top fit together.

Take time to establish an exact ¼"-wide seam guide on your machine. Some machines have a special presser foot that measures exactly ¼" from the center needle position to the edge of the foot. If your machine does not have this type of foot, place the ¼" mark of an acrylic ruler under the needle, and then create a seam guide by placing the edge of a piece of masking tape, moleskin, or a magnetic seam guide exactly ¼" to the right of the needle. If your machine has an adjustable needle-position function, you can use it in conjunction with another type of presser foot, such as the zigzag foot, and adjust the needle position to stitch ¼" from the outside edge of the foot. Always make test samples to ensure the ¼" measurement is accurate, no matter which method you use.

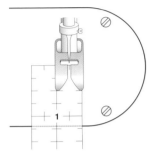

Use ¼" mark on acrylic ruler to locate a new seam guide.

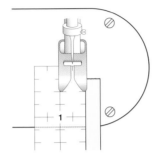

Put masking tape in front of needle along edge of ruler to guide fabric.

Making Templates

You will need to make templates for some of the pieces that cannot be rotary cut. The template patterns are given with the projects that require them. All of the patterns are full size. Depending on the technique used to stitch the pieces to the quilt, the patterns may or may not include seam allowances. The seam allowance will be shown if it has been added. Seam allowance will not be added to all of the pieces, so be sure to refer to the instructions for the appliqué method(s) indicated for each project before cutting out the pieces.

To make a template:

1. Place a piece of template plastic, or the desired template material, over the desired pattern.

2. Using a fine-point permanent marker, trace the perimeter of the shape onto the plastic. Mark the grain line and label the shape with the template letter.

3. Cut out the template on the perimeter lines.

Embellishment Basics

THIS IS THE section where you will find information on the supplies and techniques used throughout this book for embellishing the projects. Specific embellishment instructions are given for each quilt. Always read the manufacturer's instructions on supplies when applicable. And remember, your sewing-machine manual and machine dealer are great resources.

Supplies

The supplies covered here are the ones I have used in the projects, but they are just a sampling of what is available. Embellishment items and tools can be found in all sorts of places, so don't limit your search to the fabric store. Expand your imagination and look for unique items for decorating your quilts wherever you go. If you cannot find a certain item, consult "Resources" on page 79.

BUTTONS

Quilters have often been heard to say that they don't "do" buttons. Clear your mind of that philosophy for these quilts, because buttons are a great way to add texture and dimension to a quilt,

and they can be anything from whimsical to elegant. Just look at all of the button options available to you at the fabric store. There is everything from plain, round disks to zebras, and from four-hole styles to two-hole and shank styles.

Two quilts in this book use buttons as accents. In "Spring Topiary" (page 34), small flower-shaped buttons are used for the flower centers. Buttons shaped like insects were also added to complete the spring feeling. "Filbert Tree" (page 66) used a grab bag of relatively plain buttons in many colors to embellish the "leaves." The buttons are sewn on with embroidery floss, and the floss ends are tied off on the front of the quilt and left hanging to add more interest (refer to "Applying Buttons" on page 15).

While buttons were only used on two quilts, they certainly could have been used on many, if not all, of the others. Just think how "Emerald Fields" (page 30) would look with a smattering of green buttons incorporated on the pieced strips, or the effect a row of sparkling buttons would have on one of the many fabric strips in "Cinco de Mayo" (page 47). You could even use plain black buttons in the center of the sunflower heads on "Cosmic Pumpkins" (page 52) to represent the seeds. Keep thinking and I know you will find lots of ways to sneak buttons into your embellishing.

FUSIBLE TRANSER WEBS

This product is great for a multitude of needs, but it is a must for two of the appliqué techniques in

this book. Several companies manufacture transfer webs, but I prefer the HeatnBond products from Therm O Web. Make sure whatever fusible web you choose has a paper backing so the motif pattern can be traced onto it.

The type of fusible web you will need depends on the type of appliquéing you are doing. Lightweight web can be sewn through and is needed for fusible-web appliqué in which the motifs are permanently secured with stitching (refer to page 13). Heavyweight web does not require sewing and is ideal for providing the body needed for three-dimensional appliqué (refer to page 14). The materials lists for projects in which appliqué techniques are used, such as "Spring Topiary" (page 34), will specify which type(s) of web to purchase.

When using fusible webs, be sure your fabrics have been prewashed. The sizing that is added to fabrics to give them body can prevent the adhesive from adhering properly. Fabric softeners can also prevent adhesion, so avoid fabric softeners of any kind, including dryer sheets, when prewashing and drying your fabrics. As always, follow the manufacturer's instructions.

GLUE STICK

Just a dab of glue stick will temporarily keep buttons and trims in place while you are stitching them down. Select a glue that is suitable for fabric and will not gum up your needle.

HOOPS

A hoop holds the fabric taut and helps prevent puckering when you are doing machine embroidery (refer to page 18). You do not need a computerized machine to do decorative stitching, but if you are embroidering designs from a disk, use the hoop that came with your machine. Otherwise, a regular screw-type hoop or spring-tension hoop will work just fine.

Presser Feet, Bobbins, and Needles Used in Embellishment

PRESSER FEET

Sewing-machine manufacturers are constantly making sewing easier by providing presser feet for specific tasks. Feet are available for sewing on buttons by machine, couching trims, applying braids, quilting, and embroidering, to mention just a few. Specific feet will be called for in the materials section for each project whenever possible. Be sure to consult your sewing-machine dealer for feet to fit your machine; they can make sewing easier and more enjoyable.

SEWING-MACHINE NEEDLES

In addition to needles used for piecing the quilts, some of the stitching techniques and threads will require a specific type of needle to create the most desirable results. It is well worth the investment to have a supply of universal, embroidery, top-stitching, quilting, and metallic needles on hand so the right one is available when you need it.

STABILIZERS

Stabilizers are used for two reasons in this book: to support the weight of the quilt top when lots of appliqué pieces have been added to it, such as in "Cosmic Pumpkins" (page 52), and to keep the fabric from puckering when doing decorative stitching and machine embroidery, such as in "Woven Hearts" (page 24) and "Victorian Fans" (page 41).

Stabilizers come in all types, weights, and widths. The yardage requirements for the projects in this book are based on 22"-wide stabilizer. The type and weight will be indicated in the materials section for each project that uses stabilizer.

TEMPLATE MATERIAL

Templates can be made from many different materials, including plastic, cardboard, and sandpaper. It does not matter what kind of material you make your templates from as long as it is sturdy. Template plastic, which is made specifically for making templates, can be found at most fabric and quilt shops. It comes in clear, opaque, and gridded forms. Refer to "Making Templates" on page 9 for instructions on tracing and cutting out the pieces.

TEMPORARY SPRAY ADHESIVE

This timesaving product has so many uses that I do not know how I ever got along without it. Use it to hold appliqué pieces to your quilt top until they can be stitched in place, "baste" your quilt layers together, adhere stabilizer to the wrong side of the quilt top while applying decorative stitches, or hold patterns in place while cutting

them out, to name just a few. Basically, this product can take the place of many tasks that were once accomplished with pins or thread basting.

There are many temporary sprays on the market, but I prefer Sulky of America's KK 2000. Whatever brand you purchase, be sure to carefully follow the manufacturer's instructions for use. Many of the adhesives are highly flammable and must be used in well-ventilated areas. Most allow the item that was sprayed to be repositioned without spraying again, just in case it was put in the wrong spot or you decide you like it somewhere else better. Some sprays dissipate within a few hours, so you may not want to use that type if you think your project will take longer than the adhesion life of the spray.

THREADS

Naturally, you will need thread to construct the quilts, but thread is a great embellishment tool as well. Thread comes in many different weights and fibers and can greatly enhance your finished projects. Take "Happy New Year!" (page 20) for instance. Heavyweight decorative threads that were not able to go through the needle were wound onto the bobbin and couched onto the quilt during the quilting process. The added texture and color give the quilt an entirely different appearance than it would have had if the quilt had been traditionally quilted. Multiple different threads were also applied to the pieced strips of "Emerald Fields" (page 30) before and after the strips were cut. Additional interest was added by leaving strands of thread hanging off the

bottom of the quilt. Embroidery floss also can be used to stitch down buttons, such as on "Filbert Tree" (page 66).

TRIMS

Ribbons, cording, lace, soutache braid, rickrack—you name it, it can be used to embellish your quilts. Even the smallest pieces of trim can find a home in one of these projects. If it works to make your quilt special, use it.

Some trims can be applied to your projects using special presser feet, but others are easier to apply by hand. Refer to "Securing Trims" on page 19 for tips on applying these decorative accents.

Techniques

The techniques presented here are what I find easiest and what I used to make the quilts in this book. Refer to this section when indicated in the quilt instructions, or if another method works better for you, use it.

APPLIQUÉ

Three types of appliqué techniques—fusible-web appliqué, three-dimensional appliqué, and padded appliqué—were used in this book.

Fusible-Web Appliqué

This is a quick alternative to hand appliqué. You will need a lightweight fusible transfer web that can be sewn through. Heavyweight transfer web may gum up your needle, so be sure to check the package or bolt information to make sure you can sew through the product. For the top thread, you can use a thread color that either matches or contrasts with the appliqué fabric. All-purpose or rayon threads are popular choices for appliqué, but you can use any thread that will fit through the needle and provide you with the desired results. For the bobbin, use all-purpose thread or a thread designed specifically for the bobbin.

1. Trace the appropriate appliqué patterns onto the paper side of the fusible web. Trace as many of each pattern as indicated in the instructions, leaving a small amount of space between each shape. *Do not add seam allowance to the pattern.*

2. Cut out the traced shapes, leaving a ⅛" margin.

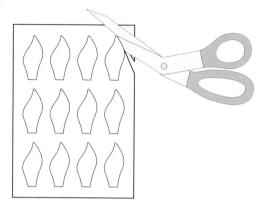

3. Follow the manufacturer's instructions to fuse each shape to the wrong side of the appropriate fabric.

4. Cut out the appliqué shapes on the drawn line. Gently peel away the paper backing from the fabric.

5. Position the appliqué shape in place according to the pattern instructions; fuse in place.

6. Place a piece of tear-away stabilizer under the fused shape. Stitch around the edges of each shape, using either a satin stitch, small zigzag stitch, or decorative stitch, such as a buttonhole stitch. You may need to adjust the upper tension slightly so the bobbin thread pulls to the underside of the appliqué and cannot be seen in the topstitching.

Three-Dimensional Appliqué

For this technique, two fabric pieces are placed wrong sides together and either fused or stitched together before being cut out. For the pieces that are fused together, use heavyweight fusible transfer web; the shapes will not be stitched to the base fabric on all of the edges and need to be stable enough to hold their shape. Pieces that are stitched together will have batting between them to provide the extra stability required.

For appliqué shapes that are fused together:

1. Remove the paper backing from the appropriate-size piece of transfer web. Place the two pieces of fabric indicated in the project instructions wrong sides together, sandwiching the transfer web between them. Follow the manufacturer's instructions to fuse the fabrics together.

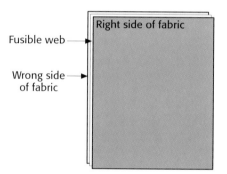

2. Refer to "Making Templates" on page 9 to trace the required template patterns onto template material. Cut out the templates.

3. Place the template on the fused fabric. Using a sharp pencil, trace around the template.

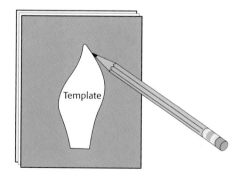

4. Cut out the shape on the drawn lines.

5. Position the motif on the quilt top and tack it in place as indicated in the project instructions.

For appliqué shapes that are stitched together:

1. Refer to "Making Templates" on page 9 to trace the required templates onto template material. Cut out the templates.

2. Place the template on the right side of the appropriate fabric. Using a sharp pencil, trace around the template.

3. Place another piece of fabric the same size as the fabric with the shape traced onto it on a flat surface, wrong side up. Layer the fabric with a piece of batting and then the fabric with the shape traced onto it, right side up.

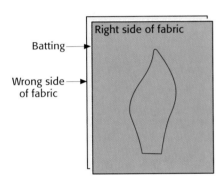

4. Using a satin stitch, stitch on the traced lines. Add any other detail stitching as indicated in the project instructions. Cut out the shape close to the stitching. If you cut into the stitching, stitch back over the cut area.

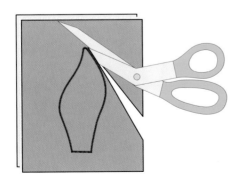

5. Position the motif on the quilt top and tack it in place as indicated in the project instructions.

Padded Appliqué

Like three-dimensional appliqué, padded appliqué provides dimension to the appliqué pieces, but the edges of the motifs are stitched to the quilt top with a decorative stitch to secure them.

1. Refer to "Making Templates" on page 9 to trace the required template patterns onto template material. Cut out the templates.

2. Place the template on the wrong side of the appropriate fabric. Using a sharp pencil, trace around the template.

3. With right sides together, layer the marked fabric with an unmarked piece of fabric of the same size. Place a piece of batting the same size as the fabric pieces on the unmarked side of the fabric pair. Straight stitch on the marked lines.

4. Using pinking shears, trim close to the stitching. With regular scissors, cut a slit in the center of the marked fabric piece. Turn the appliqué to the right side through the slit; press.

5. Position the appliqué on the quilt top as indicated in the project instructions. Using a decorative stitch, such as a blanket stitch, stitch around the appliqué edges.

APPLYING BUTTONS

Buttons can be applied by machine or by hand, whichever you prefer. Use a glue stick to hold the button in place temporarily while you stitch it down.

You do not always have to use matching thread to stitch the buttons in place. Try rayon or metallic thread to give an added spark to plain buttons, or use embroidery floss and tie the thread tails in a knot on the quilt front like I did for "Filbert Trees" (page 66).

BOBBIN WORK

Bobbin work is a technique used to apply heavy threads that will not go through a needle, as well as some narrow cords, to the right side of the fabric. The thread or cord needs to be narrow enough that it can be wound onto the bobbin and come up through the bobbin hole in the throat plate; if it is not, you will need to use couching techniques (refer to "Couching" on page 17). Because the decorative thread will be coming from the bobbin, the design is sewn with the wrong side of the work facing up.

"Happy New Year!" (page 20) is the only quilt in this book that specifically calls for the bobbin-work technique, but you could certainly use the technique to add accents to other projects. Because the bobbin work in "Happy New Year!" is part of the quilting process, a walking foot was used to feed the layers through the machine evenly. If you choose to do bobbin work on a single layer, such as a quilt top, a regular zigzag foot will work just fine.

To do bobbin work, follow these instructions:

1. Place the bobbin on the bobbin winder and hold the decorative thread in your hand, or if the thread is on a spool or cone, let it reel off a pencil held in front of the bobbin winder. Wind at an even speed, guiding the thread with your fingers. You can also wind the bobbin by hand, but be sure to wind the thread evenly onto the bobbin and do not twist the thread.

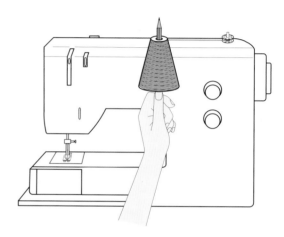

2. Thread the machine with all-purpose or decorative thread in a color that matches or contrasts with the background fabric.

3. Insert the bobbin into the machine, referring to your sewing-machine manual for advice

on using thicker threads in the bobbin. Generally you will be instructed to adjust the tension guide so the thread will flow easily through the slit with just a slight tension on it. It is a good idea to have an extra bobbin case on hand for this purpose so that you won't need to readjust your bobbin for regular sewing when you are finished with the bobbin work. For some machines, you will be instructed to bypass the tension all together. Turn the hand wheel to bring the bobbin thread to the top.

4. Test stitch on materials that are similar to those in your quilt. Place the fabric, wrong side up, under the needle. Select a stitch that does not create a buildup of thread. A satin stitch would not be appropriate, but a straight stitch, wide zigzag stitch, or feather stitch would work well. To begin stitching, pull the bobbin thread to the fabric surface. You may need to lengthen the stitch length to achieve the desired results. The top tension should not need adjusting. Leave a long bobbin tail when you end stitching, and then thread it through a large-eye needle and pull it to the back; tie the bobbin and top thread in a knot, at both the beginning and end, to secure them. An exception to this is "Happy New Year!" which is couched from edge to edge. The decorative thread ends are trimmed when you square up the quilt.

COUCHING

In couching, the decorative thread or trim is laid on the fabric surface and stitched over to secure it. The trim does not go in the needle or bobbin. You can use this technique to apply any type of thread, yarn, ribbon, or other trim to the surface of a fabric. The technique was used in "Emerald Fields" (page 30) to apply all of the trims and threads. Because the trims were laid on the fabric surface, they could be left hanging off the edge.

You can use a zigzag stitch, serpentine stitch, or other decorative stitch to secure the trim; use whatever works best to secure the trim and provide the effect you want. Any thread can be used as well. If you want the trim to stand out on its own, use an invisible thread. Use a contrasting thread and a decorative stitch to add dimension and interest.

There are several presser feet available to make the couching process easier, although a zigzag foot will work with most stitches. Consult your sewing machine dealer about using other feet, such as an embroidery foot, tricot foot, braid and piping foot, open-toe appliqué foot, or cording foot in conjunction with the couching technique.

To couch, follow these instructions:

1. Select a presser foot appropriate for the trim and stitch width and attach to the machine. Select the thread for the top and insert the appropriate needle into the machine. Thread the needle with the selected thread and wind the bobbin with matching all-purpose thread.

2. Test stitch on materials that are similar to those in your quilt. Lay the desired thread or trim on the fabric surface. Select a stitch and adjust the width so the stitch will span the trim. Stitch over the trim, adjusting width and tension, if necessary, to achieve the desired results.

DECORATIVE STITCHING

Throughout this book you will see many references to decorative stitching. Basically, a decorative stitch is any stitch that is not a straight stitch. Even some utility stitches, such as a three-step zigzag, can be classified as decorative if they provide the effect you want. Be as fancy or as subdued as you want to achieve the desired results. It is entirely up to you!

Depending on the stability of your base fabric, you may need to add a tear-away stabilizer to the fabric wrong side. Test stitch on fabric scraps, with and without stabilizer, to see what works best. A hoop may also be necessary to hold the fabric taut.

MACHINE EMBROIDERY

There are several different ways to do machine embroidery, and there is enough relevant information available to fill books, so I will keep it simple here. The machine embroidery on the projects in this book were all done on a Husqvarna Viking Designer I machine. This computerized sewing-and-embroidery machine stitches motifs from a special disk that is inserted into the machine. A hoop in which you place your fabric and stabilizer is attached to the machine to hold the fabric taut and move the hoop in the directions needed to complete the design. All I have to do is select the design and threads and place the fabric in the

Machine Embroidery Tips

- Preshrink the fabric you are using for the background of the embroidered design.

- Use a new embroidery needle. Some of the designs have more than 10,000 stitches per design. When the needle becomes dull, the design can become distorted.

- Use a lightweight thread in the bobbin, such as Sulky's Lightweight Bobbin Thread. Choose white or black, depending on the color of the background fabric. If needed, change the bobbin thread color when you change the needle thread color. It is also efficient to pre-wind several bobbins.

- There are many different types of fabric stabilizers. I prefer a tear-away stabilizer under the fabric when I machine embroider on a standard cotton quilting fabric. Sometimes a liquid stabilizer works well when a fabric is light in color or weight. If you find that you need more stability to keep the fabric from puckering, try using a water-soluble or heat-soluble stabilizer.

- Make sure the stabilized fabric is in the hoop on grain, if possible, and has no puckers or pleats. The fabric should be taut, but not pulled so tight that it stretches. The hoop keeps the fabric from moving, which is important when stitching the designs.

- Stitch out a test of the desired embroidery design. Use the background fabric and the threads and stabilizer product you intend to use for the project. This will show you if the thread tension is correct, if the thread coverage is sufficient, and the actual look of the embroidered design on the background fabric. Make adjustments if necessary. Use any embroidered samples that are not quite perfect as labels, or incorporate them into the backing.

hoop so the motifs are stitched where I want them; the machine does the rest. The machine stops stitching when the thread needs to be changed. If you have such a machine, consult your sewing-machine dealer and manual for specific instructions.

If you do not have a machine that does embroidery, never fear. Many of the other embellishing techniques discussed in this section can be substituted with spectacular results. Take "Victorian Fans" (page 41) for instance. Decorative stitching, whether completed by hand or machine, can easily be substituted for many of the stitches. Couch on trims or use bobbin-work techniques for more variety. Appliqués and buttons could also provide texture and dimension. Use the supplies and tools you have and personalize the design to your own specifications.

SECURING TRIMS

As we discussed previously, some trims can be couched in place. I normally use a wide zigzag stitch and an open-toe appliqué foot to stitch them in place. Other trims may need to be hand stitched. It will just depend on the thickness of the trim and any decorative accents that may be on the trim. For either method, I temporarily adhere the trims using a dab of glue stick or wash-away double-sided tape, such as Wonder Tape, on the trim's wrong side. The only exception to this is if the trim is transparent, such as a chiffon ribbon; I pin those trims in place.

If the ends of your trims, like the trims on "Cinco de Mayo" (page 47), will not be caught in a seam, be sure to treat them with a seam sealant before you stitch them in place so that they will not ravel, or turn the trim ends under and stitch them in place. Tape the ends of any leftover trims that ravel.

You can use various threads for attaching trims. I use a clear monofilament thread on decorative three-dimensional trims so the thread will not interfere with the design on the trim. On plain trims that I want to enhance, I often stitch them down with a matching rayon or cotton thread and a decorative stitch. It is usually best to have the bobbin thread color match the needle thread.

I love to embellish. The patchwork on a quilt—or in some cases on a wearable—is the canvas for me. I do patchwork so that I have a surface for the embellishment. Very often I have the embellishment pieces and need to create the patchwork on which to feature the special embellishments. These pieces tell a story. I collect embellishing items everywhere: shells on the beach, old discarded costume jewelry, keys, cuff links, tie tacks from my father-in-law's old dresser drawer, beads and trinkets from the craft store, sequined appliqués from a flea market, antique postcards and pictures for photo transfer, and odds and ends from someone's junk stash. The list could go on and on, including the obvious things such as threads and buttons found in a quilt shop. I love to make use of old, considered unusable, stuff in my home, so this just carries over to the work I do, too.

Judy Murrah
Author

Happy New Year!

Like the fireworks that light up the sky as the new year is welcomed, this wall hanging offers a sprinkling of color against the darkness of night. And it couldn't be easier; four-patch units, solid squares, and half-square-triangle units are assembled into rows to create the starry design. Make it twinkle with the addition of novelty threads that are applied during the quilting process. Select an assortment of heavier threads and yarns for the bobbin-work technique, as well as decorative threads that can be used in the needle, to give the wall hanging dimension and texture.

FINISHED QUILT SIZE: 31" x 35"

Materials

Yardage is based on 42"-wide fabric.

- ¾ yard of white print for background
- ⅝ yard of black print for outer border
- ½ yard of black polished cotton for stars
- ¼ yard *total* of assorted bright solids for four-patch units
- ¼ yard of yellow solid for inner border
- 1 yard of fabric for backing
- ½ yard of fabric for binding
- Craft-size batting (36" x 46")
- Assortment of decorative heavyweight threads for bobbin-work quilting
- Extra bobbin case (optional, but recommended if you have a machine with a removable bobbin case)
- Walking foot

Cutting

From the white print, cut:

- 3 strips, 2⅞" x 42"
- 1 strip, 2½" x 42"; crosscut the strip into 15 squares, 2½" x 2½"
- 4 strips, 1½" x 42"; crosscut the strips into 84 squares, 1½" x 1½"*

From the black polished cotton, cut:

- 3 strips, 2⅞" x 42"
- 1 strip, 2½" x 42"; crosscut the strip into 15 squares, 2½" x 2½"

From the assorted bright solids, cut a *total* of:

- 42 pairs of squares (84 total), 1½" x 1½"*

From the yellow solid, cut:

- 4 strips, 1¼" x 42"

From the black print, cut:

- 4 strips, 4" x 42"

From the binding fabric, cut:

- 4 strips, 3" x 42"

*If you are making several four-patch units using the same bright color, follow the tip after step 3 of "Assembling the Wall Hanging Top" to cut the white and bright color pieces required for the four-patch units.

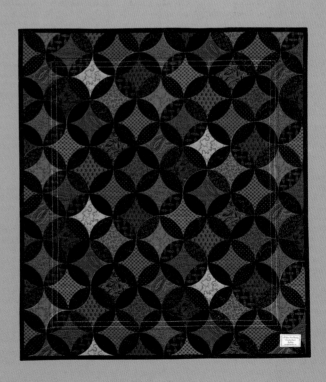

DESIGN DETAIL

Choose a large-scale geometric print for the backing, like the one shown below. Quilt by following the lines of the design rather than marking the backing fabric.

Assembling the Wall Hanging Top

1. To make the half-square-triangle units, place each white 2⅞" x 42" strip right sides together with a black 2⅞" x 42" strip. From the paired strips, cut 36 squares, 2⅞" x 2⅞". With the fabrics still together, cut each square in half once diagonally. Discard one paired set of triangles.

2. Stitch the paired triangles together along the long edges. Press the seam toward the black triangle. Make 71 half-square-triangle units.

Make 71.

3. To make the four-patch units, stitch each white 1½" square to a bright solid 1½" square. Stitch two identical segments together as shown. Make 42 four-patch units.

Make 42.

TIP

If you are making several four-patch units using the same bright color, cut 1½"-wide strips from the bright color and pair each strip with same-length white 1½"-wide strips. Stitch the strips together along the long edges to make a strip set; then crosscut the strip set into 1½"-wide segments.

4. Assemble the half-square-triangle units, the four-patch units, and the white and black 2½" squares into rows as shown. Stitch the units in each row together. Press the seams in alternate directions from row to row. Stitch the rows together. Press the seams in one direction.

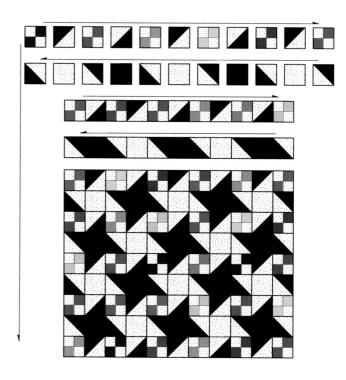

Finishing the Wall Hanging

Refer to "Quilt Finishing" on pages 73–78.

1. Sew the yellow strips to the top and bottom of the quilt top and then to the sides. Press the seams toward the borders. Repeat with the black print strips for the outer border.

2. If you are not using a backing fabric with a design that you can follow for quilting, mark the backing with the desired design.

3. Layer the quilt top with batting and backing; baste.

4. Referring to "Bobbin Work" on page 16, wind the extra bobbin with one of the heavier novelty threads. Attach the walking foot to the machine and thread the needle with the desired thread. Working from the quilt backing side, stitch as much of the quilting design as desired with that bobbin thread; then change to another decorative thread. Continue stitching and changing threads until the desired effect is achieved.

5. Bind the edges of the quilt.

6. Add a hanging sleeve and label if desired.

Before computerized embroidery, I found such satisfaction teaching free-motion embroidery across America. From letters I have received over the years, it's amazing to me the way a skill like free-motion embroidery could change so many people's lives. Women and men alike have found that they do indeed have a creative nature and that they can express it through thread work. Many used the skill as a therapeutic tool to recover from the hurt of divorce, loss of a loved one, depression, or a serious illness. Now with the advent of the computer age, everyone can be an expert at embroidery by machine and share their joy with others. The technology of new threads, stabilizers, and computerized sewing machines has opened up a revolution of creative expression in machine embroidery. Sewing is no longer viewed only as a way to mend or alter clothing. Now sewing represents a creative outlet for people from 6 to 86!

Joyce Drexler
Executive Vice President and
Creative Director,
Sulky of America, Inc.

Woven Hearts

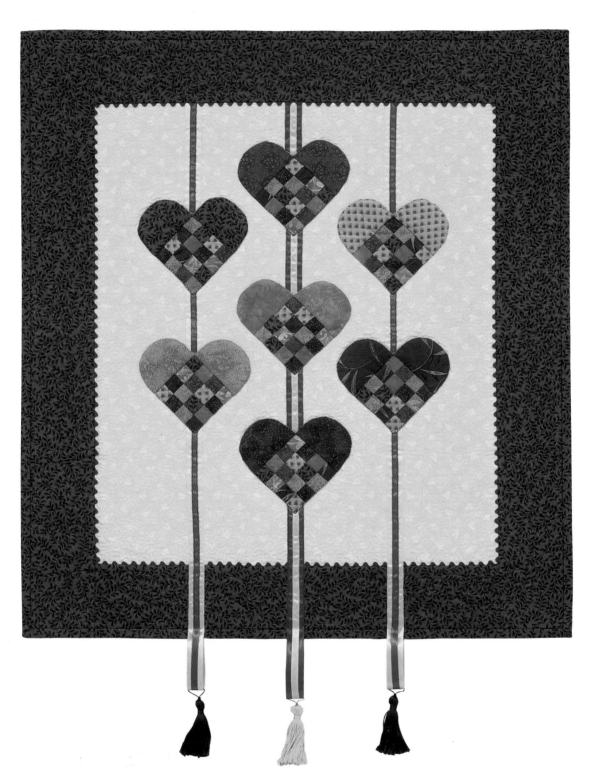

By M'Liss Rae Hawley; machine quilted by Barbara Dau. Inspired by a Victorian bell pull, this is a wonderful wall hanging for Valentine's Day, an anniversary, or for a baby's nursery. Simply change the color of the background, border, and heart fabrics to suit the occasion; then find some great ribbons and tassels to complement the new look.

FINISHED QUILT SIZE: 29" x 32"

Materials

Yardage is based on 42"-wide fabric.

- ¾ yard of yellow fabric for background
- ⅝ yard of purple fabric for border
- ¼ yard of purple solid for heart lining
- ⅛ yard *each* of 8 assorted purples and fuchsias for hearts
- 1 yard of fabric for backing
- ½ yard of fabric for binding
- Craft-size batting (36" x 46")
- ⅞"-wide double-faced satin ribbon: 2 yards of yellow; 1 yard of purple
- ⅜"-wide double-faced satin ribbon: 1 yard of yellow; 2 yards of purple
- Rayon threads to match rickrack and ribbons
- 2 packages of purple medium rickrack (2½ yards per pkg.)
- 3"-long tassels: 2 purple; 1 gold or yellow
- Template plastic
- 1 yard of 22"-wide tear-away stabilizer
- Temporary spray adhesive
- Fabric glue stick

Cutting

From the 8 assorted purples and fuchsias, cut a *total* of:
- 8 strips, 1¼" x 20"; cut each strip in half widthwise to make 16 strips, 1¼" x 10"

From 7 of the 8 assorted purples and fuchsias, cut from *each*:
- 2 template A pieces (page 29)

From the purple solid for heart lining, cut:
- 7 squares, 6½" x 6½"

From the yellow fabric, cut:
- 1 rectangle, 22" x 25"

From the purple fabric for border, cut:
- 4 strips, 4" x 42"

From the binding fabric, cut:
- 4 strips, 3" x 42"

Making the Heart Appliqués

1. Stitch together four assorted purple and fuchsia strips to make a strip set. Press the seams in one direction. Make four strip sets total. From the strip sets, cut 28 segments, 1¼" wide.

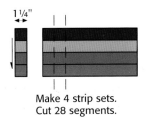

Make 4 strip sets.
Cut 28 segments.

2. Stitch four different segments from step 1 together along the long edges to make a sixteen-patch block. Make seven total, varying the position of like strips between the blocks to make each one different. Press the seams in one direction.

Make 7.

3. Stitch two matching template A pieces to two adjacent sides of each sixteen-patch block as shown. Press the seams toward the A pieces. Make seven total.

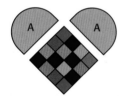

Make 7.

4. With right sides together, position each heart on a purple 6½" square; press together and then pin in place. Stitch ¼" inside the edge of each heart, using a shorter-than-normal stitch length. Press again. Trim the lining fabric even with the edge of each heart. Clip the curved edges.

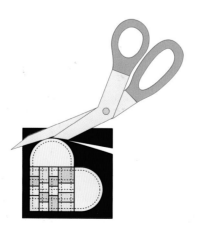

TIP

To make the edges smoother when you turn the hearts, use pinking shears to trim the lining fabric rather than clipping the curved edges.

5. Gently pull on the lining at the center of each heart to separate it from the pieced top; cut a small slit in the center of the lining. Turn each heart to the right side through the lining slit, gently pushing out the curves from the inside; press. Make seven lined hearts.

Assembling the Wall Hanging Top

1. To mark the ribbon placement lines, use the marking tool of your choice to mark the vertical center on the right side of the yellow rectangle. Measure 5½" on each side of the line and mark another line that runs parallel to the center line. To mark the rickrack placement lines, measure ¼" from the rectangle outer edges. Pin the stabilizer to the rectangle wrong side, or follow the manufacturer's instructions to adhere it with temporary spray adhesive.

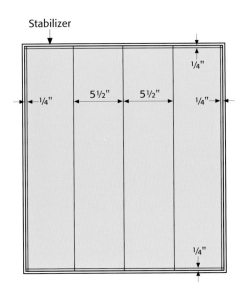

2. Cut the 2-yard-long ribbon pieces into 1-yard lengths. Lightly apply glue stick to the ribbon placement lines. With right sides up and upper edges aligned, center the ⅞"-wide purple ribbon on the center line and a ⅞"-wide yellow ribbon on the remaining two lines, allowing the excess to hang off the bottom edge of the rectangle. Using matching rayon thread, stitch along both long edges of each ribbon, stopping 2" from the bottom of the rectangle. Center the opposite-color ⅜"-wide ribbon over each of the ⅞"-wide ribbons. Lightly apply glue stick to the wrong side of each ribbon to keep it in place, but do not apply it to the portion of the ribbon that hangs off the edge of the fabric. Stitch down the narrow ribbons in the same manner as the wider ribbons.

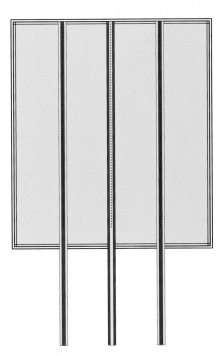

Add stitching to center of ribbons.
End stitching 2" from quilt bottom edge.

3. From the rickrack, cut two pieces slightly longer than the rectangle's top and bottom edges and two pieces slightly longer than the sides. Center the top and bottom rickrack pieces over the top and bottom marked lines,

placing the rickrack over the ribbons at the top edge and under the ribbons at the bottom edge; pin or glue the trim in place. Temporarily lay the side rickrack pieces in place; adjust the top and bottom pieces, if necessary, so the rickrack at the corners falls as desired. Remove the side pieces. Pin the loose ribbons at the lower edge out of the way of the stitching lines. Using matching thread, stitch the rickrack in place, following the marked line. Stitch the side rickrack pieces in place in the same manner. Trim the rickrack ends even with the quilt edges.

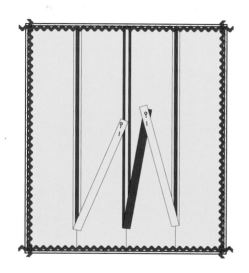

TIP

Before you stitch the rickrack to the quilt, test the machine tension by stitching a scrap of rickrack to a scrap of the background fabric. If the rickrack gathers or puckers, reduce the tension until the problem is eliminated.

4. Spray the lined side of the pieced hearts with temporary spray adhesive. Carefully center the hearts over the ribbons on the background rectangle as shown, and finger-press them into place. Set up the machine to sew a blanket stitch. Using matching thread, stitch around the edges of each heart. Remove the stabilizer from the background rectangle.

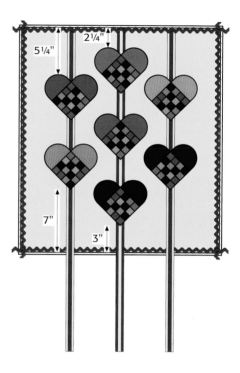

TIP

For another look, stitch one purple and one fuchsia template A piece to each sixteen-patch block.

Finishing the Wall Hanging

Refer to "Quilt Finishing" on pages 73–78.

1. Sew the purple border strips to the top and bottom edges of the quilt top and then to the sides. Press the seams toward the borders.

2. Layer the quilt top with batting and backing; baste.

3. Quilt the background as desired, being careful not to stitch over the ribbons, rickrack, or hearts.

4. Bind the edges of the quilt.

5. Trim the two side ribbons 6" from the quilt bottom edge and the center ribbon 7" from the bottom edge. Place each ribbon end through the hanging loop of a tassel. Fold under the ribbon ends ½"; then hand stitch the folded edges to the back of the quilt, 1" from the quilt bottom edge.

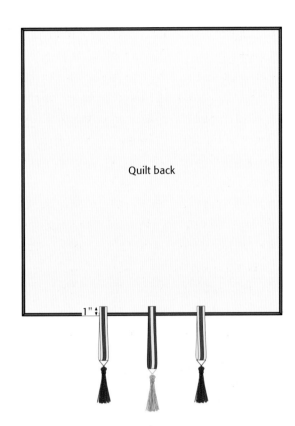

6. Add a hanging sleeve and label if desired.

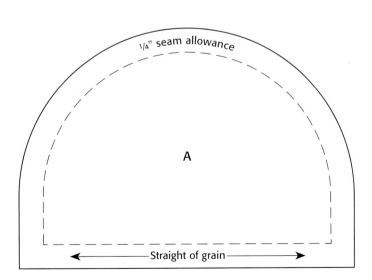

Emerald Fields

Embellish patchwork strips with ribbons, threads, and decorative stitching to create a wall hanging as lush and breathtaking as the fields of Ireland. The pieced strips are made by laying an assortment of medium- and dark-value green strips over a lighter green base fabric in such a way that the base fabric is visible. Decorative stitching and trims are then used to embellish the strips and adhere them to the base fabric. The resulting fabric is then cut into strips across the fabric, and those strips are then applied to the background fabric using more decorative stitching and trims.

FINISHED QUILT SIZE: 30" x 41"

Materials

Yardage is based on 42"-wide fabric.

- 7/8 yard *total* of 12 assorted medium and dark green fabrics for pieced strips
- 3/4 yard of off-white fabric for background
- 5/8 yard of light green fabric for base of pieced strips
- 5/8 yard of blue-and-green fabric for outer border
- 1/4 yard of light gold fabric for inner border
- 1 3/8 yards of fabric for backing
- 1/2 yard of blue-green fabric for binding
- Craft-size batting (36" x 46")
- Assorted colors of cotton, rayon, and metallic threads for couching trims and embellishing pieced strips
- Approximately 2 yards *each* of an assortment of 1/2"-wide-or-less ribbons, cords, trims, and laces for couching to pieced strips
- Temporary spray adhesive (optional)
- Seam sealant
- Walking foot or open-toe appliqué foot

DESIGN DETAIL

A lightweight upholstery fabric is ideal for the background of this quilt. It is just heavy enough to support the extra weight of the pieced fabric strips without adding bulk to the finished wall hanging. A suitable alternative would be a sturdy, medium-weight cotton.

Cutting

From the off-white fabric, cut:
- 1 rectangle, 22" x 33"

From the light green fabric, cut:
- 1 rectangle, 18" x 34"

From the assorted medium and dark green fabrics, cut a *total* of:
- 1 strip, 1 1/2" x 20"
- 3 strips, 1 5/8" x 20"
- 2 strips, 2" x 20"
- 1 strip, 2 1/4" x 20"
- 2 strips, 2 1/2" x 20"
- 3 strips, 2 5/8" x 20"

From the light gold fabric, cut:
- 4 strips, 1" x 42"

From the blue-and-green fabric, cut:
- 4 strips, 4" x 42"

From the blue-green fabric, cut:
- 4 strips, 3" x 42"

Making the Pieced Strips

1. On the right side of the light green 18" x 34" rectangle, use a pencil to mark a line 2" from and parallel to each 18"-long edge. Lay a 1 5/8" medium to dark green strip along each of the drawn lines so that the strip's 20" edge is positioned along the drawn line and about 1" of excess strip extends beyond each

long edge of the base fabric as shown. Pin the strips in place, or follow the manufacturer's instructions to use the spray adhesive to temporarily adhere the strips to the base fabric.

2. Lay the remaining medium to dark green strips between the two strips from step 1 as shown. Leave about ¼" to ½" of base fabric visible between each strip and make sure the strips are straight and parallel to each other. Pin or spray-baste the strips in place; then thread-baste along their long edges.

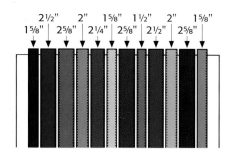

3. Now, the fun begins! Using threads in colors similar to the background, stitch rows of decorative stitches the length of each strip. Add as many rows to each strip as desired, referring to "Couching" on page 17 to incorporate a piece of trim occasionally. Be sure to add decorative stitching and trims to some of the base fabric that is visible between the strips.

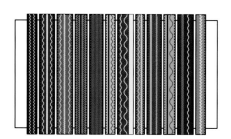

4. When you have achieved the desired effect, remove the basting stitches. Press the fabric from the right and wrong sides.

5. Straighten one long edge and both ends of the pieced base fabric. Trim the short edges. Crosscut the fabric into the following strips: two strips, 2¼" wide; three strips, 2" wide; one strip, 1¾" wide; and one strip, 1½" wide. Set the strips aside.

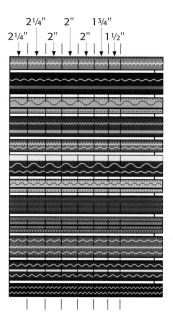

Assembling and Finishing the Wall Hanging

Refer to "Quilt Finishing" on pages 73–78.

1. Sew the light gold inner borders to the top and bottom edges of the off-white 22" x 33" rectangle and then to the sides. Press the seams toward the borders. Repeat with the blue-and-green strips for the outer border.

3. Layer the quilt top with batting and backing; baste.

4. Using a variety of threads and decorative stitches, begin at the top of each strip and stitch the length of the strip. Because you are quilting as you go, you will need to use either a walking foot or an open-toe appliqué foot. Add as many rows to each strip as desired, referring to "Couching" on page 17 to incorporate as many trims to each strip as desired. End stitching at the bottom of each strip, leaving as much as 6" of each thread and trim extending beyond the outer border. Apply seam sealant to the ends of each thread and trim to keep them from raveling.

2. Position the pieced strips on the quilt top as shown, staggering each one slightly. Make sure the strips run parallel to each other and the side borders. You may place the strips so that the fabrics in each strip are in the same order, or you may turn them so some strips are running in the opposite direction. Pin or spray-baste the strips in place; then thread-baste along the strip long edges.

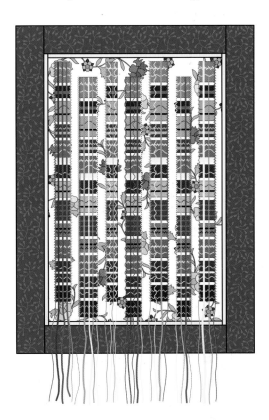

5. When you are satisfied with the embellishment, quilt the background and borders as desired.

6. Bind the edges of the quilt.

7. Add a hanging sleeve and label if desired.

Spring Topiary

Celebrate spring and all its freshness with this delightful topiary that's guaranteed to attract lots of spectators. Kick your imagination into gear and you will be able to enjoy the sights, sounds, and even the smell of this wonderful season year-round. This quilt is a great project if you want to learn about products and techniques that make three-dimensional machine appliqué fast and fun.

FINISHED QUILT SIZE: 28½" x 43½"

Materials

Yardage is based on 42"-wide fabric.

- 1½ yards of dark green fabric 1 for outer border
- ¾ yard of beige print for pieced background top
- ½ yard of medium green fabric 1 for vine and leaves
- ⅜ yard of medium green fabric 2 for pieced background bottom
- ⅜ yard of medium green fabric 3 for tree head
- ¼ yard of orange fabric for inner border
- ¼ yard of brown fabric for tree trunk
- ¼ yard *each* of 2 terra cotta fabrics for pot inner strips
- ⅛ yard of terra cotta fabric that coordinates with inner strips for pot outer strips
- 5" x 10" rectangle of tulle in a color to match multicolor print for butterfly
- 4" x 8" rectangle of multicolor print for butterfly
- Scraps of assorted purples, oranges, and yellows for topiary flowers and tulips
- Scraps of assorted green fabrics for leaves and tulip stems
- 1½ yards of fabric for backing
- ½ yard of dark green fabric 2 for binding
- Crib-size batting (45" x 60")
- Fourteen ½"-diameter buttons for flower centers
- 1¼ yards of 22"-wide tear-away stabilizer
- Template plastic
- Fusible transfer web: ⅜ yard each of lightweight and heavyweight fusible transfer web
- Temporary spray adhesive

DESIGN DETAIL

It is important to use a batting that can help support the weight of this quilt. With the addition of so many appliqué pieces, the wall hanging needs a batting that is heavier than what you would use for a traditionally pieced, unembellished quilt of this size. My recommendation would be Quilters Dream Batting Select Loft.

Cutting

From the beige print, cut:
- 1 rectangle, 19½" x 27½"

From the medium green fabric 2, cut:
- 1 rectangle, 7" x 19½"

From *each* of the 2 terra cotta fabrics for the pot inner strips, cut:
- 2 strips, 2½" x 42"

From the terra cotta for the pot outer strips, cut:
- 1 strip, 2½" x 42"

From the brown fabric, cut:
- 1 strip, 2½" x 12"

From the medium green fabric 1, cut:
- 1 strip, 1½" x 20", along the bias grain

From the orange fabric, cut:
- 3 strips, ¾" x 42"

From the dark green fabric 1, cut:
- 2 strips, 5" x 22", along the lengthwise grain
- 2 strips, 5" x 45½", along the lengthwise grain

Assembling the Wall Hanging Top

1. With right sides together, sew the beige and medium green fabric 2 rectangles together along the 19½" edges. Press the seam toward the green rectangle.

2. To make the three-dimensional, double-sided topiary flowers and leaves, refer to "Three-Dimensional Appliqué" on page 14 to fuse a flower scrap to another flower scrap, wrong sides together, using heavyweight fusible web. Leave some scraps unfused for the A, D, and E pieces that will be cut out in step 4. You do not have to fuse the same fabrics together, but it is a good idea to fuse each scrap to one of the same color. Repeat with the leaf scraps, using the same two fabrics for the scraps that will be for the tulip leaves (I and I reversed).

3. Trace patterns B, C, F, G, H, I, and I reversed on page 40 onto template plastic; cut them out. Using the templates and a sharp pencil, trace 14 of B and 11 of C onto the fused flower scraps and cut them out. The A, B, and C flowers will be stacked on top of each other, so you may want to plan ahead so you have one purple, one orange, and one yellow flower in each group, not necessarily in the same order (the A flowers will be cut out in step 4). Repeat with the fused leaf scraps to make 30 of F and 20 *each* of G and H. Cut three of I and one of I reversed from the same fabric. Also from the fused leaf fabrics, cut one strip, ⅜" x 3", and one strip, ⅜" x 2¼", for the tulip stems. Set the fused pieces aside.

4. Referring to "Fusible-Web Appliqué" on page 13 and using the patterns on page 40, trace 2 of D and 2 of E onto the paper side of the lightweight fusible web. Also draw a 10"-diameter circle for the topiary head. Fuse the A shapes to the unfused topiary flower scraps, the D shapes to the tulip background fabric scraps, and the E shapes to the tulip fabric. Fuse the circle to the topiary head fabric. Remove the paper backing and set the shapes aside.

5. To make the pot, fold each of the five terra cotta 2½" x 42" strips in half lengthwise, wrong sides together, aligning the raw edges. Stitch ¼" from the long edges. Lay each strip on an ironing surface with the seam centered on the strip; press the seam open as you press the strip flat.

TIP

Press the strips on a tailor's ham or seam roll to minimize the seam imprint on the right side.

6. From two strips of one of the inner colors, cut seven segments, 7" long. From the remaining two inner-color strips, cut six segments, 8" long. From the outer-color strip, cut two segments, 6½" long, and two segments, 9½" long.

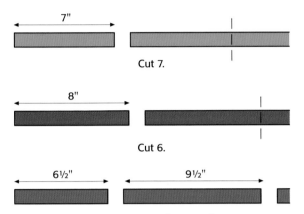

Cut 7.

Cut 6.

Cut two 6½" segments and two 9½" segments.

7. Cut an 8½" x 9" rectangle of stabilizer. Draw a straight line, parallel to and ½" from the 8½"-long edge. Position the ends of the seven inner-color 7"-long segments along the drawn line, placing the strips vertically side by side; baste in place along the upper edge of the strips. Weave the 8"-long strips horizontally through the vertical strips, using an over-one, under-one pattern. Keep the strips as close together as possible to eliminate any show-through. When all the strips are in place, stitch ½" from the edges. Carefully remove the stabilizer.

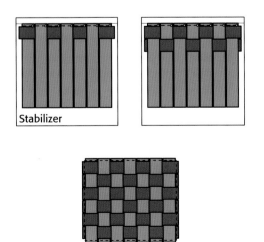

8. Position stabilizer on the wrong side of the pieced backing. Secure it in place with pins or temporary spray adhesive.

9. Center the woven piece 3¼" from the bottom edge of the green background rectangle and 6¼" from the pieced background sides; pin in place.

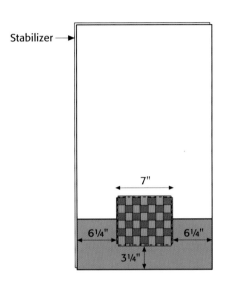

10. Press under the ends of each of the pot outer-color strips ¼". Position the 6½" strips along the sides, placing the inner edge just barely onto the edges of the woven strips, as shown. Topstitch along both long edges. Stitch a 9½" strip along the bottom edge in the same manner, stitching along all of the edges. Set the remaining outer-color strip aside. It will be stitched in place after the tulips, trunk, and vine have been stitched in place.

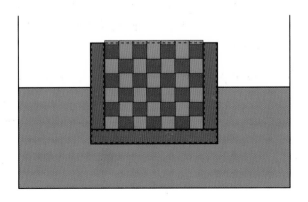

11. Fold the brown strip in half lengthwise, wrong sides together, aligning the raw edges. Stitch ¼" from the long edges. Repeat with the medium green 1 bias strip, using an ⅛" seam allowance. Referring to step 5, press the seams open. Center one end of the brown strip just slightly above the woven pot upper edge with the seam against the background; pin in place. Beginning slightly above the woven piece and referring to the photo, wind the green strip over and under the brown strip; pin in place. Using matching thread, carefully stitch along both long edges of the brown strip, ending stitching when you reach a portion of the green strip that crosses over the brown strip; lock the stitches, clip the thread, and continue stitching on the other side of the green strip.

12. Randomly tuck one tip of each vine leaf (H) under the green strip. Using matching thread, stitch along both edges of the green strip, ending stitching when you reach a portion of the green strip that goes under the brown strip; lock the stitches, clip the thread, and continue stitching on the other side of the brown strip.

13. Position the tulip stems on the background so they just touch the woven piece as shown. Using a decorative stitch, stitch through the center of the stems. Follow the manufacturer's instructions to fuse a tulip background shape (D) that was cut out in step 4 to the top of each stem, overlapping the stem end slightly. Center a fused tulip shape (E) to each background tulip; pin in place. Using matching thread, straight stitch ⅛" from the tulip edges. Position the tulip leaves on each side of the tulips as shown. Using a decorative stitch and matching thread, stitch the leaves

in place, leaving approximately 1" unstitched at the leaf tips.

14. Referring to step 10, position the remaining pot outer-color strip at the pot upper edge, covering the ends of the trunk, tulip leaves and stems, and the edges of the woven strips. Topstitch along all of the edges.

15. Follow the manufacturer's instructions to center and fuse the topiary head circle to the top of the trunk, overlapping the end of the trunk slightly. Using a decorative stitch and matching thread, stitch around the circle.

16. Position the C flower shapes from step 3 on the topiary head. Randomly tuck the tip of each large and small flower leaf (F and

G) under the flowers, referring to the photo if desired. Follow the manufacturer's instructions to fuse the flowers in place, securing the leaves at the same time. Layer each C flower shape with a fused B flower shape and then a fused A flower shape, rotating the shapes to stagger the petal positions; pin in place. Pin the remaining three fused B flower shapes to the head as desired. Stitch through the center of the layered flower shapes and the B flower shapes about ½" to secure them to the head.

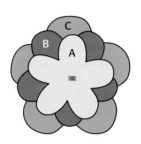

17. To make the butterfly, spray the wrong side of the butterfly fabric rectangle with temporary adhesive. Fold the rectangle in half, wrong sides together, to make a 4" x 4" square. Trace pattern J on page 40 onto template plastic; cut it out. Referring to "Three-Dimensional Appliqué" on page 14, use the template and a pencil or fabric marker that is visible on the fabric to trace the shape onto the folded square. Place a piece of stabilizer under the folded square. Using a coordinating thread, satin stitch over the traced lines. Remove the stabilizer. Cut the excess fabric

away, close to the stitching line. Fold the tulle rectangle in half to make a 5" x 5" square. Center the butterfly on the tulle square and pin it in place. Stitch around the butterfly, just inside the satin stitching. Cut away the excess tulle ¼" from the butterfly edges. Set aside the butterfly.

18. Carefully remove the stabilizer from the back of the quilt top.

Finishing the Wall Hanging

Refer to "Quilt Finishing" on pages 73–78.

1. Refer to "Adding Borders" on page 73 to cut and sew the orange ¾"-wide strips to the top and bottom edges of the quilt top and then to the sides. Press the seams toward the borders. Cut the dark green 5" x 22" strips to fit the top and bottom edges of the quilt; stitch in place. Repeat with the 5" x 45½" strips and stitch them to the quilt sides.

2. Layer the quilt top with batting and backing; baste.

3. Quilt as desired.

4. Bind the edges of the quilt with the dark green fabric 2 strips.

5. Stitch a button to the center of each flower on the topiary head. Position the butterfly on the background where desired. Straight stitch through the center of the body, leaving the wings free.

6. Add a hanging sleeve and label if desired.

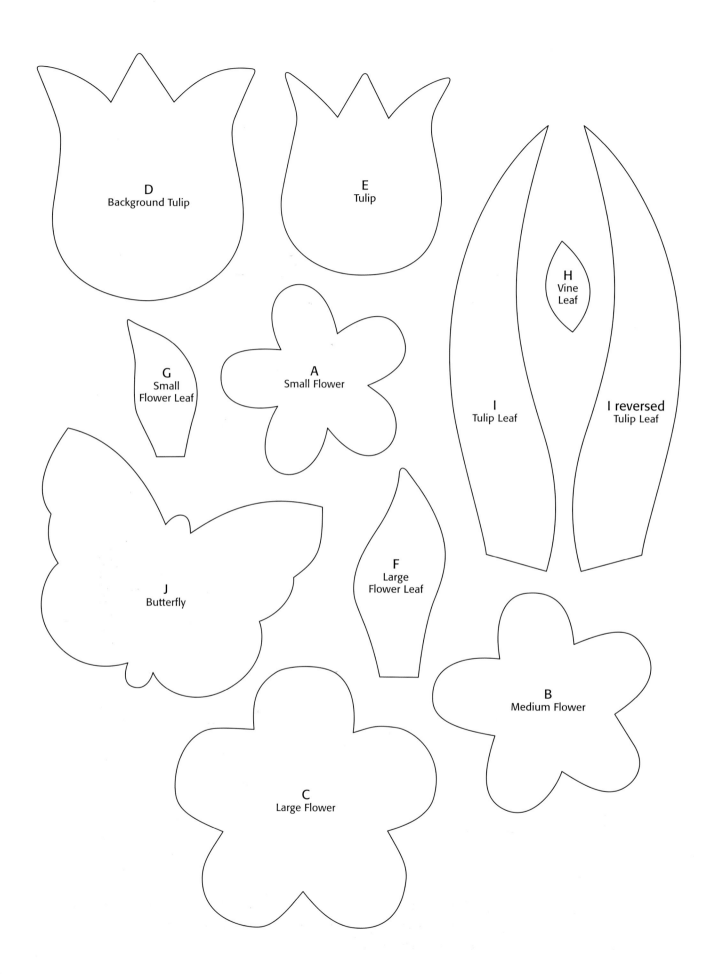

D
Background Tulip

E
Tulip

H
Vine
Leaf

G
Small
Flower Leaf

A
Small Flower

I
Tulip Leaf

I reversed
Tulip Leaf

J
Butterfly

F
Large
Flower Leaf

B
Medium Flower

C
Large Flower

Victorian Fans

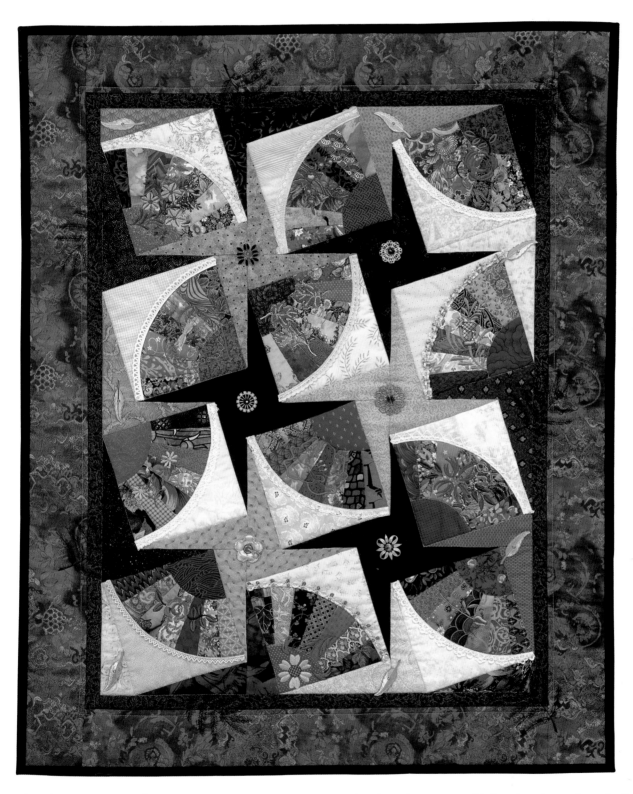

One of my favorites, this old-fashioned block gets a new twist when wedge-shaped pieces are added to the sides, making the fans appear to dance. This quilt offers a great opportunity to use some of your smaller fabric scraps and to show off your machine-embroidery skills. Add to the romance with lace, costume jewelry, and beads.

FINISHED QUILT SIZE: 30" x 37"

Materials

Yardage is based on 42"-wide fabric.

- ⅝ yard of dark multicolor fabric for outer border
- ¼ yard of dark green fabric for inner border
- ⅛ yard *each* or scraps of 10 assorted black fabrics for block side wedges
- ⅛ yard *each* or scraps of 10 assorted dark gold fabrics for block side wedges
- Scraps of 12 assorted burgundy fabrics for fan quarter-circles
- Scraps of assorted medium to dark fabrics for fan blades
- Scraps of 12 assorted light pink fabrics for fan backgrounds
- 1 yard of fabric for backing
- ½ yard of fabric for binding
- Craft-size batting (36" x 46")
- Twelve 10" lengths *total* of assorted laces and trims for embellishing fan arcs
- Assorted threads for machine embroidery
- Assorted jewelry and beads for embellishing
- Template plastic
- Stabilizer
- Hoop for machine embroidery

Cutting

From the assorted medium to dark scraps, cut a *total* of:

- 84 template B pieces (page 46)

From *each* of the 12 assorted burgundy fabrics, cut:

- 1 template A piece (12 total) (page 46)

From *each* of the 12 assorted light pinks, cut:

- 1 template C piece (12 total) (page 46)

From *each* of 3 of the assorted black fabrics, cut:

- 4 template D pieces (12 total) (page 46)

From *each* of 5 of the remaining assorted black fabrics, cut:

- 2 template D pieces (10 total)

From *each* of the remaining 2 assorted black fabrics, cut:

- 1 template D piece (2 total)

From *each* of 3 of the assorted dark gold fabrics, cut:

- 4 template D pieces (12 total)

From *each* of 5 of the remaining assorted gold fabrics, cut:

- 2 template D pieces (10 total)

From *each* of the remaining 2 assorted gold fabrics, cut:

- 1 template D piece (2 total)

From the dark green fabric, cut:

- 4 strips, 1¼" x 42"

From the multicolor fabric, cut:

- 4 strips, 3" x 42"

From the binding fabric, cut:

- 4 strips, 3" x 42"

Assembling the Wall Hanging Top

1. Stitch seven template B pieces together along the long edges as shown. Press the seams in one direction. Make 12.

Make 12.

2. Fold each template A piece in half along the curved edge to find the center; use a pin to mark the center point. Repeat to mark the center of both curved edges of the pieced template B sections and the curved edge of the template C pieces.

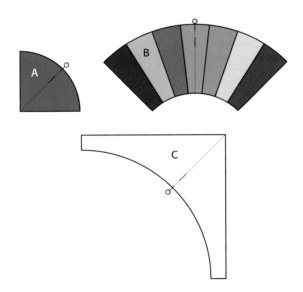

3. With right sides together, match the template A center point to the concave-curved-edge center point of each pieced template B section. Pin the pieces together at the center points. Gently manipulate the pieced B section to fit the A section, matching raw edges and pinning as you go. With the B section on top, stitch the pieces together. Press the seam toward the A piece. Make 12.

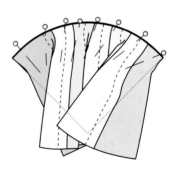

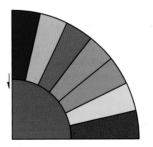

Make 12.

4. Referring to step 3, pin a C piece to each convex-curved edge of the pieced B sections, matching center points. With the C piece on top, stitch the pieces together. Press the seam toward the C piece. Make 12.

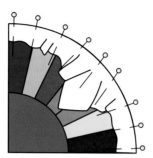

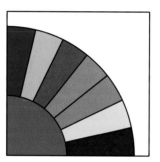

Make 12.

5. Arrange the pieced squares in four rows of three blocks each, tipping them slightly to mimic the position of the blocks in the finished quilt. Rotate the blocks as desired so the A pieces are in different corners. Position two gold template D pieces and two black template D pieces on opposite edges of each square as shown so that when the resulting blocks are sewn together, the areas where four adjacent wedges meet will form a star. Be sure that the wedges that form a star are made up of the same fabric.

6. To finish each block, stitch the gold template D pieces to the block first. Be sure the template D pieces are stitched exactly as they were positioned in step 5. Press the seams toward the template D pieces. Stitch the black template D pieces to the remaining two sides. Press the seams toward the template D pieces. Make 12.

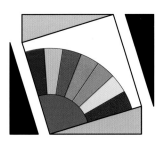

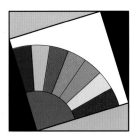

Make 12.

7. Rearrange the blocks exactly as they were positioned in step 5. Sew the blocks in each row together. Press the seams in opposite directions from row to row. Stitch the rows together. Press the seams in one direction.

Finishing the Wall Hanging

Refer to "Quilt Finishing" on pages 73–78.

1. Stitch the dark green strips to the top and bottom of the quilt top and then to the sides. Press the seams toward the borders. Repeat with the multicolor strips.

2. Refer to "Machine Embroidery" on page 18 to embroider the blocks with the desired motifs.

3. Layer the quilt top with batting and backing; baste.

4. Quilt as desired.

5. Stitch the jewelry and beads or any other desired trims, including the lace on the fan arcs, to the quilted top.

6. Bind the edges of the quilt.

7. Add a hanging sleeve and label if desired.

I love the way embellishment has become "sew" creative! Years ago when I would show garments that had frayed fabric pieces embellishing them, many people would look at the garment and often touch it (they couldn't keep their hands off of it!) and say, "Tacky, tacky!" Today it is not only acceptable to have "strings" of thread and other embellishments hanging from garments, it is considered fiber art!

Sue Hausmann, Senior Vice President of Education and Consumer Motivation, Husqvarna Viking

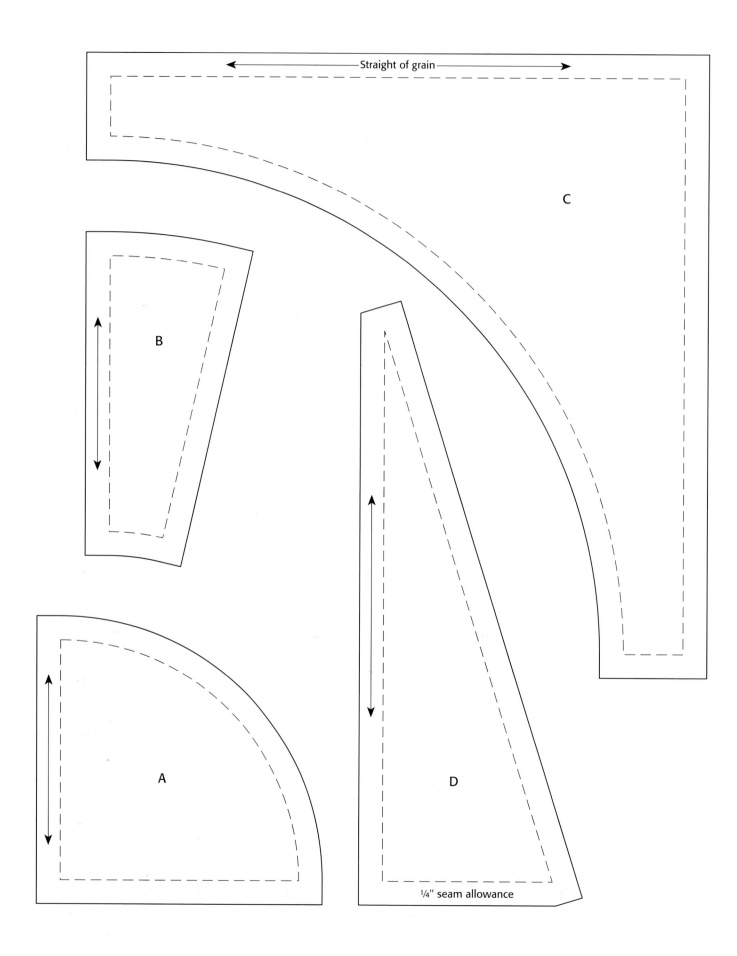

Straight of grain

C

B

A

D

¼" seam allowance

Cinco de Mayo

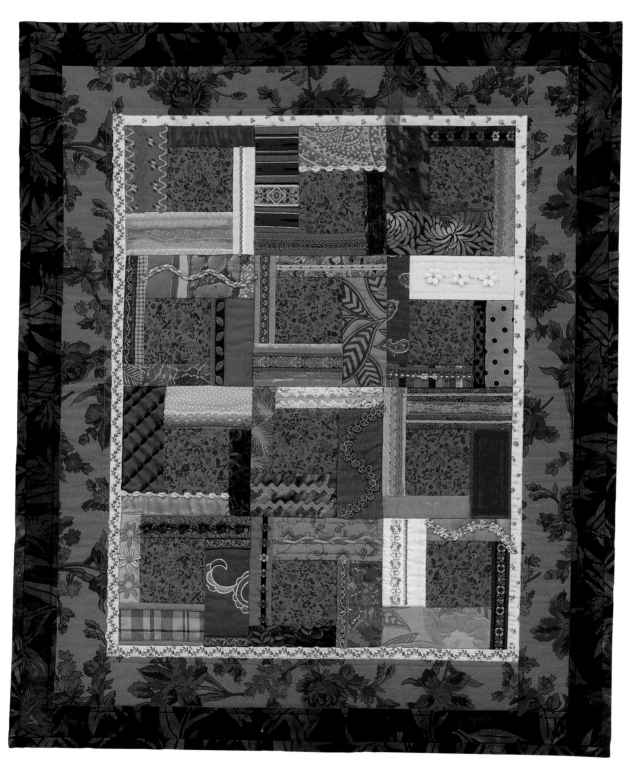

Viva el Cinco de Mayo! May 5, 1862, is the day the Mexican army defeated the French at the Battle of Puebla. Although the victory was short-lived for Mexico, it is symbolic of the country's fight for self-rule, which eventually happened in 1867. Today, colorful celebrations, complete with mariachi music, parades, and dancing, are held in Mexico and America to commemorate the liberty and freedom that were achieved on that day.

FINISHED QUILT SIZE: 28½" x 34½"

Materials

Yardage is based on 42"-wide fabric.

- ¾ yard *total* of assorted bright scraps for blocks
- ⅜ yard of bright fabric 1 for block centers
- ⅜ yard of bright fabric 2 for middle border
- ⅜ yard of bright fabric 3 for outer border
- ¼ yard of bright fabric 4 for inner border
- 1 yard of fabric for backing
- ½ yard of bright fabric 5 for binding
- Craft-size batting (36" x 46")
- Assorted trims for embellishing blocks and inner border

DESIGN DETAIL

My "Cinco de Mayo" quilt is made entirely of bright fabric scraps from my children's clothes, old curtains, blanket bindings, velvet from my sister-in-law's 1965 prom dress, and my husband's ties, but you could easily interpret the design to suit other occasions. For instance, you may want to make a wedding or memory quilt for an anniversary. Instead of bright fiesta-color fabrics, use white and beige with beautiful lace and ribbon trims that continue the theme. Replace the center block with one that has had a photo transferred to fabric. Or go with fabrics that complement a baby theme, sports theme, or any other idea you might have. It will look great!

Cutting

From the bright fabric 1, cut:
- 2 strips, 3½" x 42"; crosscut the strips into 12 squares, 3½" x 3½"

From the assorted bright scraps, cut a *total* of :
- 12 rectangles, 1½" x 4½"
- 12 rectangles, 1½" x 5½"
- 12 rectangles, 2½" x 4½"
- 12 rectangles, 2½" x 5½"

From the bright fabric 4, cut:
- 3 strips, 1" x 42"

From the bright fabric 2, cut:
- 3 strips, 2¾" x 42"

From the bright fabric 3, cut:
- 4 strips, 2½" x 42"

From the bright fabric 5, cut:
- 4 strips, 3" x 42"

TIP

You may want to consider stitching certain flat trims or laces to the rectangles before you add them to the block center square.

Assembling the Wall Hanging Top

1. Attach a 1½" x 5½" rectangle to the top edge of each bright fabric 1 block center. Begin stitching at the upper-left-hand corner and end 1" from the upper-right-hand corner; backstitch. Press the seam toward the rectangle.

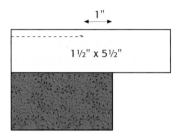

2. Working counterclockwise, stitch a 1½" x 4½" rectangle of a different color to the left-hand side of each block. Press the seam toward the rectangle.

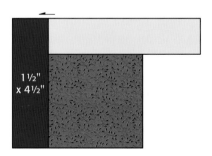

3. Stitch a 2½" x 4½" rectangle to the bottom edge of each block. Press the seam toward the rectangle.

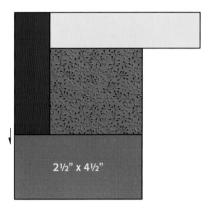

4. Stitch a 2½" x 5½" rectangle to the right-hand side of each block, being careful not to catch the rectangle from step 1 in the seam. Press the seam toward the newly attached rectangle. Stitch the unstitched portion of the strip from step 1 to the center square and the end of the 2½" x 5½" strip to complete the block. Press the seam toward the step 1 rectangle. Make 12 blocks.

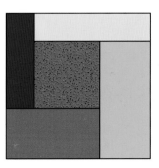

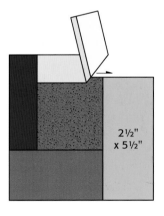

Make 12.

5. Arrange the blocks into 4 rows of 3 blocks each, rotating the blocks in each row as shown. Stitch the blocks in each row together. Press the seams in opposite directions from row to row. Stitch the rows together. Press the seams in one direction.

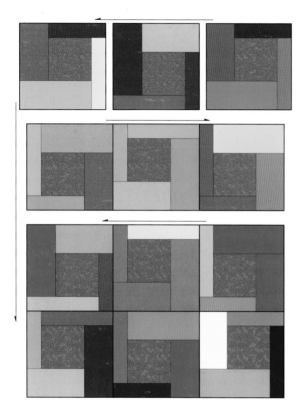

Finishing the Wall Hanging

Refer to "Quilt Finishing" on pages 73–78.

1. Sew the inner borders to the top and bottom edges of the quilt top and then to the sides. Press the seams toward the border. Repeat for the middle and outer borders.

2. Layer the quilt top with batting and backing; baste.

3. Stitch in the ditch around each piece of fabric in the quilt to stabilize the piece for the addition of the trims. Stitch ¼" from the middle- and outer-border seam lines.

4. Refer to "Securing Trims" on page 19 to stitch the assorted trims to the block rectangles and borders as desired, leaving the center square in each block unembellished.

5. Quilt any of the remaining unembellished block rectangles as desired. I stippled some pieces and used a decorative stitch on others. On some rectangles, I used the fabric pattern as my quilting guide. I did not quilt the center square of each block.

6. Bind the edges of the quilt.

7. Add a hanging sleeve and label if desired.

> There are no rules in this game; your imagination is the only limitation.
>
> *Maurine Noble*
> *Author*

Trim Placement and Application Tips

There is no right or wrong way to apply your trims to this quilt, but you may want to consider some of the following options. Use one or all of the ideas, but whatever you decide, have fun!

- **Get complementary.** Choose a trim that is a complementary color of the fabric rectangle on which you will apply it. Complementary colors are ones that are directly opposite each other on the color wheel. For instance, place a piece of orange lace on a rectangle of blue fabric.

- **Go tone-on-tone.** Lay two different sizes and colors of orange rickrack on an orange fabric.

- **Pick a theme.** You can find trims with all sorts of motifs woven into or printed onto them. Stitch the trim to a coordinating solid fabric to set it off.

- **Incorporate contrast.** You will have some trims that you want to stand out more than others. By placing them on a piece of fabric that has the opposite color value, you can achieve this effect. For instance, place a black trim on a pale yellow fabric, or a light pink trim on a navy blue fabric. If you want to be more subtle, go for low contrast by applying trims that are the same tone or in the same color family as the fabric.

- **Tie the knot.** Add texture and interest to a delicate trim, such as a chiffon ribbon, by tying knots in the ribbon at 1" intervals before stitching it to the fabric.

- **Pile on the layers.** Layered trims also add a touch of the unexpected. Try layering a narrow ribbon over a wider ribbon of the same color and using a decorative stitch and rayon thread to adhere them to the quilt. Or, stitch a decorative ribbon over a piece of lace, leaving the lace edges free.

Cosmic Pumpkins

Walk through our garden under towering sunflowers. Feast your eyes on the perfect pumpkin patch! Filled with potential jack-o'-lanterns in all shapes and sizes and radiating with the cheerfulness of bright sunflowers, this patch will have you struggling to keep your hands to yourself. Well, who says you have to? The three-dimensional aspects of this wall hanging are hard to resist, and so are all the appliqué methods you will use to make it so appealing.

FINISHED QUILT SIZE: 24" x 32"

Materials

Yardage is based on 42"-wide fabric.

- 1 yard of dark purple, black, or navy fabric for background
- ¾ yard *total* of assorted yellow fabrics for sunflower petals
- ½ yard *total* of assorted green fabrics for leaves and stems
- ½ yard of brown fabric for pumpkin stems and sunflower centers
- ⅜ yard *total* of assorted orange fabrics for pumpkins
- 1 yard of fabric for backing
- ¾ yard of fabric for binding
- Crib-size batting (45" x 60")
- Cotton and rayon threads in an assortment of browns, yellows, oranges, greens, and black for stitching details and appliquéing
- 1 yard of green ¾"-wide double-faced satin ribbon
- Seam sealant
- 1 yard of plastic-covered wire
- Template plastic
- Pinking shears
- Tweezers
- 3 yards of heavyweight interfacing
- Temporary spray adhesive
- 26" x 36" piece of pattern tracing material

DESIGN DETAIL

This wall hanging has a piece of heavyweight interfacing incorporated into the layering process to give the foundation enough stability to support the weight of all of the appliqués. You should also use a heavier-weight batting than you normally would, such as Quilters Dream Batting Select Loft. Because the layers are heavier than usual, machine quilting is recommended.

Cutting

From the background fabric, cut:
- 1 rectangle, 28" x 36"

From the backing fabric, cut:
- 1 rectangle, 28" x 36"

From the batting, cut:
- 1 rectangle, 28" x 36"
- 3 rectangles, 6" x 7"
- 3 template A pieces (page 61)
- 8 template B pieces (page 61)
- 10 template C pieces (page 61)
- 12 template D pieces (page 61)
- 13 rectangles, 4" x 8"
- 9 squares, 5½" x 5½"
- 2 rectangles, 6½" x 9"
- 3 squares, 7" x 7"

From the brown fabric, cut a *total* of:
- 6 rectangles, 6" x 7"
- 2 rectangles, 3" x 8"

From the assorted yellow fabrics, cut a _total_ of:

- 12 strips, 2½" x 42"

From the assorted green fabrics, cut a _total_ of:

- 3 strips, 1" x 24"
- 3 strips, ¾" x 24"
- 3 strips, ½" x 24"
- 26 rectangles, 4" x 8"
- 18 squares, 5½" x 5½"

From the assorted orange fabrics, cut a _total_ of:

- 4 rectangles, 6½" x 9"
- 6 squares, 7" x 7"

Preparing the Wall Hanging Foundation

1. Apply the interfacing to the wrong side of the background fabric, following the manufacturer's instructions and piecing as necessary. Referring to "Layering and Basting" on page 74, layer the interfaced background piece with batting and backing, using the temporary spray adhesive between each layer to baste them together.

TIP

If the interfacing is not fusible, use the temporary spray adhesive to baste it in place.

---

2. Using an overall quilting pattern, such as stippling, quilt the layers together.

3. Enlarge the arch pattern on page 60 onto pattern tracing material and cut it out.

4. Pin the pattern to the quilted fabric and cut out the quilt foundation.

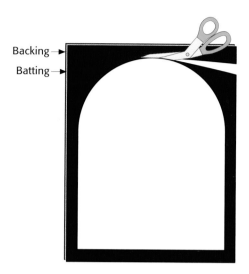

Backing →
Batting →

5. Measure around the quilt edges and cut enough bias strips from the binding fabric to equal the measurement plus 15". Referring to "Binding" on page 75, bind the foundation edges.

Making the Appliqués

1. _To make the sunflowers,_ trace template A onto the wrong side of three brown 6" x 7" rectangles. Place the batting 6" x 7" rectangles on a flat surface. Layer each of the batting rectangles with an unmarked brown 6" x 7" rectangle and then a marked brown 6" x 7" rectangle. Stitch on the marked lines of each layered rectangle.

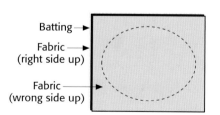

Batting →
Fabric →
(right side up)

Fabric →
(wrong side up)

2. Using pinking shears, trim close to the stitching. With regular scissors, cut a 2½"-long slit in the center of the top fabric oval. Turn each oval to the right side through the slit; press. Make three.

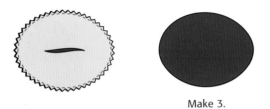

Make 3.

3. Layer each yellow strip right sides together with a different yellow strip. Trace a *total* of 18 template B shapes, 18 template C shapes, and 20 template D shapes onto the top layer of the strip pairs, leaving at least ¼" around the edges of each shape for seam allowance. Trace each template onto several different strips so you will have a variety of fabrics in the finished petals. Stitch on the marked line of each petal, leaving the straight bottom edge open. Using pinking shears, trim each petal close to the stitching edges. Turn the petals to the right side; press.

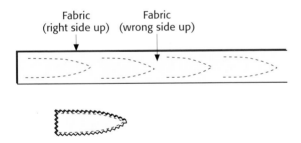

Fabric (right side up)   Fabric (wrong side up)

4. Using the tweezers, insert the template B, C, and D batting pieces into the appropriate petals through the opening, trimming the petals if needed to fit. Not every petal will have batting.

5. Topstitch around the curved edges of each petal, using a variety of yellow threads. Use a walking foot on the stuffed petals and the foot you normally use for straight stitching on the unstuffed petals. Set the petals aside.

6. For the sunflower leaves, trace template E onto the right side of five green 4" x 8" rectangles. Trace template F onto the right side of eight green 4" x 8" rectangles. Use several different fabrics for each leaf template to create interest in the finished quilt. Trace some of the leaves off-grain so they will turn in a realistic fashion when they are stitched to the wall hanging. Place the remaining green 4" x 8" rectangles on a flat surface, wrong sides up. Layer each one with a batting 4" x 8" rectangle and then a marked 4" x 8" rectangle, using spray adhesive to secure the layers together temporarily. Be sure the marked rectangle is a different fabric than the bottom rectangle.

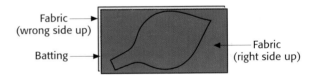

Fabric (wrong side up)   Fabric (right side up)   Batting

7. Wind the bobbin with a green cotton thread that matches the bottom fabric of one of the layered leaf rectangles from step 6; thread the needle with a rayon thread that matches the marked fabric. Satin stitch along the marked lines. Beginning at the center of the leaf base, satin stitch vein lines into the leaf, tapering each vein to a point before you reach the edge of the leaf.

TIP

Begin to taper the stitching about midway up each leaf vein. End with a point before you reach the outer edges; stitch in place to lock the threads. Try to vary the veins in each leaf for a more realistic effect.

8. Using a sharp pair of scissors, cut along the outer row of satin stitching. If you accidentally cut into the stitching, stitch back over the area. Set the leaves aside.

9. *To make the pumpkins,* trace one template I pumpkin onto the wrong side of two orange 6½" x 9" rectangles. Trace one each of templates J, K, and L onto the wrong side of three orange 7" x 7" squares. With right sides together, layer each marked rectangle and square with an unmarked square or rectangle of the same size. Place a corresponding batting piece on the unmarked side of each fabric pair; pin the layers together. Stitch on the marked lines.

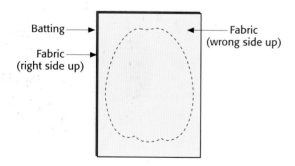

10. Using pinking shears, trim close to the stitching. With regular scissors, cut a 2½"-long slit in the center of the top fabric piece. Turn each pumpkin to the right side through the slit; press. Set the pumpkins aside.

11. Referring to steps 6–8, make the pumpkin leaves. Trace five template G leaves and four template H leaves onto the right side of the green 5½" squares. Layer each marked square with a 5½" batting square and an unmarked green 5½" square. Satin stitch the leaf veins first, extending the lines all the way to the outer leaf edges without tapering the stitch. Satin stitch around the outer edges of each leaf. Cut out each leaf along the outer row of satin stitching. Set the leaves aside.

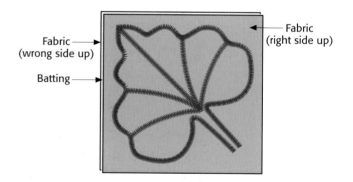

12. To make the pumpkin stems, trace one each of templates M, N, and O, and two of template M reversed onto the wrong side of one of the brown 3" x 8" rectangles. Place the remaining brown 3" x 8" rectangle on the marked rectangle, right sides together. Stitch on the marked lines. Using pinking shears,

trim close to the stitching. With regular scissors, cut a small slit in the center of one of the stem layers. Turn each stem to the right side through the slit; press. Set the stems aside.

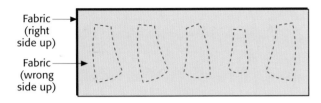

Applying the Appliqués

1. Layer each green 1" x 24" strip with a ¾" x 24" strip and then a ½" x 24" strip. Position the layered strips on the quilted foundation, placing the outer stems approximately 2" from the binding at the foundation bottom edge and the middle stem approximately 3" from the bottom edge. Stitch through the center of each strip, using a different decorative stitch for each one.

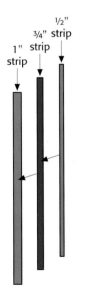

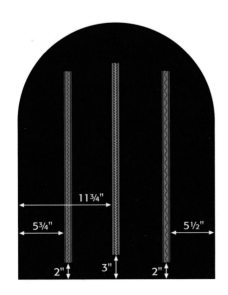

Layer strips.

2. Position a sunflower center over the top end of each stem. Trace around each center or use pins to mark the placement. Remove the centers.

3. Place all but two of the sunflower leaves under the stem edges, arranging them as desired; pin in place. Using a variety of green threads, stitch rows of decorative stitches the length of each stem. It doesn't matter how many rows you add and you do not have to stitch exactly on the edges, but you do need to make sure each leaf is secured by the stitching. Straight stitch along the center vein of each leaf, using a thread color that matches the vein satin stitching.

4. Arrange the sunflower petals and the two remaining sunflower leaves around the marked centers as desired, placing the open ends of the petals and leaves approximately ½" inside of the marked areas. Be sure to use all three petal sizes for each flower. When you are satisfied with the arrangement, pin, machine baste, or spray-baste the petals in place.

5. Trim the template A batting pieces so that they are slightly smaller than the inside of the sunflower center. Spray-baste the batting pieces and position one in the center of each sunflower head, staying inside the petal ends. Cover each of the batting pieces with a sunflower center; pin in place. Using a walking foot and brown thread, blanket stitch around the edge of each center piece.

6. Arrange the pumpkins and pumpkin leaves along the bottom edge of the quilt as desired. Remove and set aside any leaves that are not under a pumpkin; then baste the remaining pieces in place using your preferred basting method. Using a walking foot and orange thread, blanket stitch the edges of each pumpkin, stitching the pumpkins that fall behind another pumpkin first. Straight stitch the detail lines, referring to the patterns. Reposition the leaves that were on top of the pumpkins. Using a straight stitch and matching thread, tack the leaves in place so that the majority of the leaf edges are free.

7. Position the appropriate stem at the center top of each pumpkin. Using brown thread and a walking foot, straight stitch the stems to the pumpkins, leaving the portion that extends beyond the pumpkin free.

8. Fold the ribbon in half lengthwise and stitch close to the edges. Cut the piece into three 12" lengths. Knot one end of each ribbon length and apply seam sealant to the knotted end. Insert the wire through the open end of one ribbon length. Trim the wire to the same length as the ribbon. Repeat for the remaining two ribbon pieces. Wrap each wired ribbon around a pencil to create a tendril; remove the pencil.

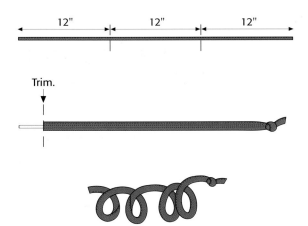

9. Place the unknotted end of a tendril under the stem of three of the pumpkins. Tack the tendril in place under the stem; then position the tendril as desired on the pumpkin and background. Tack the tendril in place at the knotted end and at any other point necessary.

10. Add a hanging sleeve and label if desired.

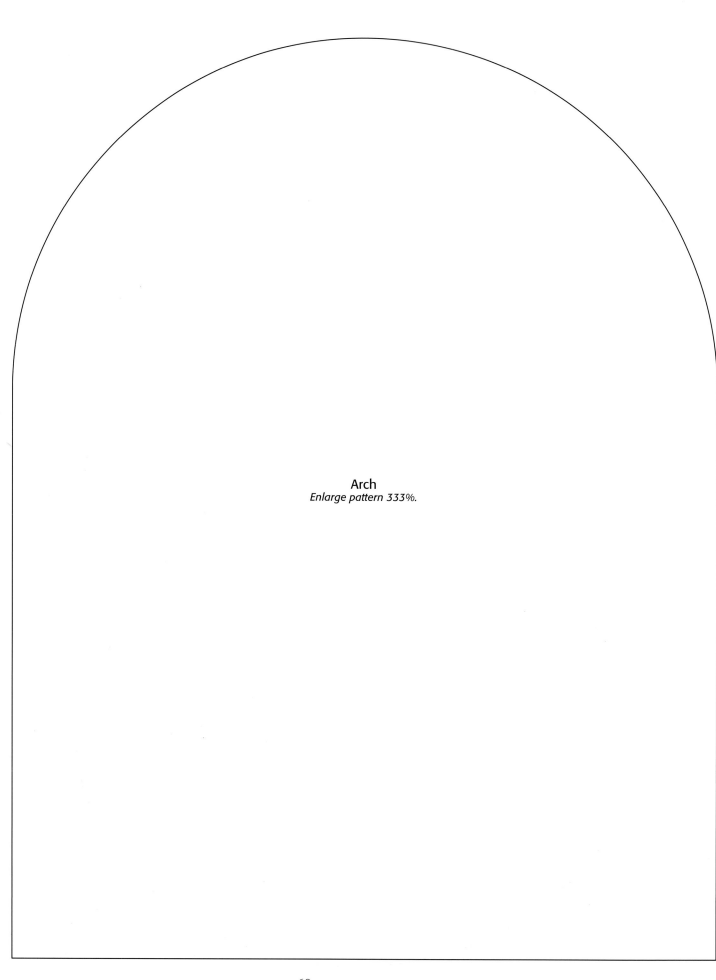

Arch
Enlarge pattern 333%.

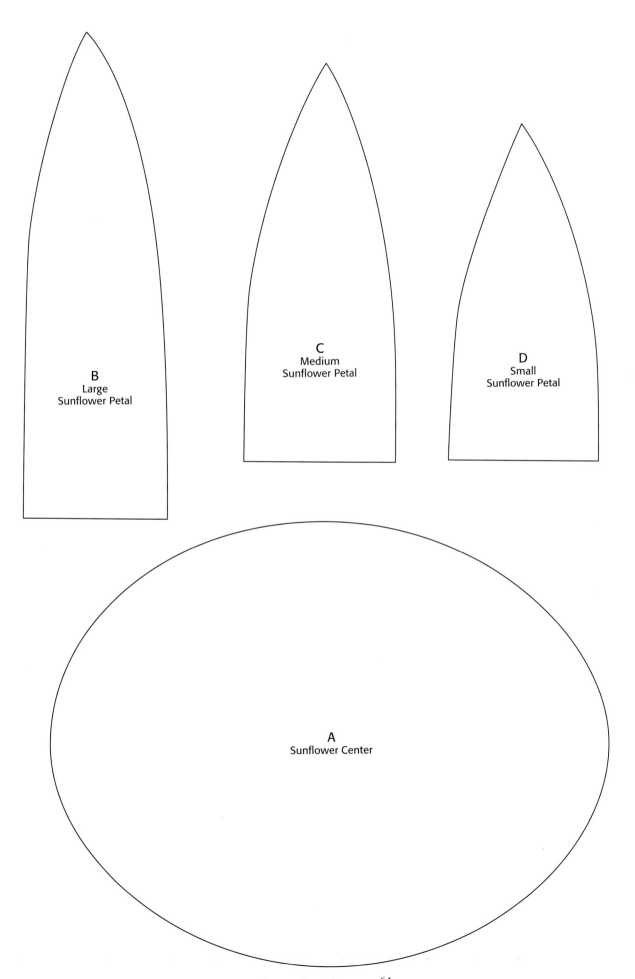

B
Large
Sunflower Petal

C
Medium
Sunflower Petal

D
Small
Sunflower Petal

A
Sunflower Center

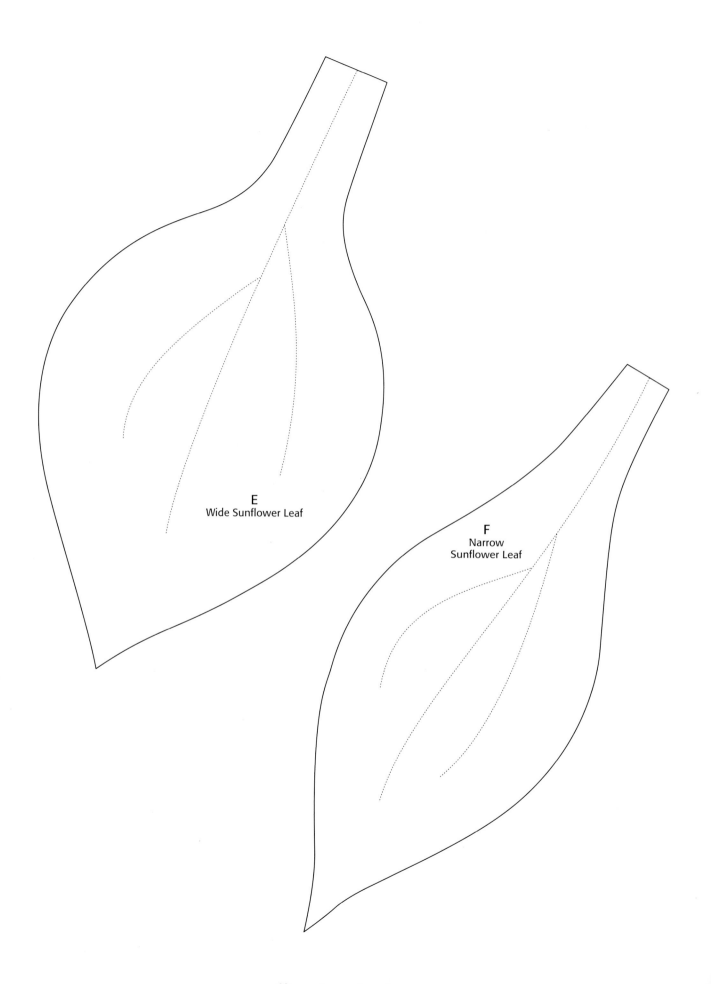

E
Wide Sunflower Leaf

F
Narrow
Sunflower Leaf

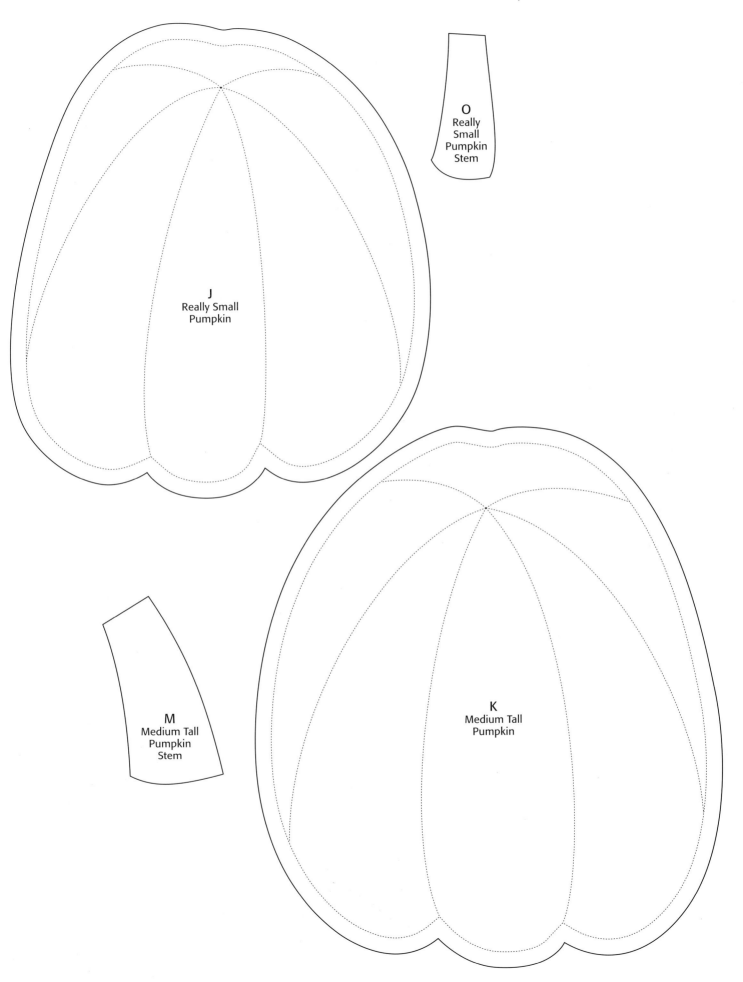

O
Really
Small
Pumpkin
Stem

J
Really Small
Pumpkin

M
Medium Tall
Pumpkin
Stem

K
Medium Tall
Pumpkin

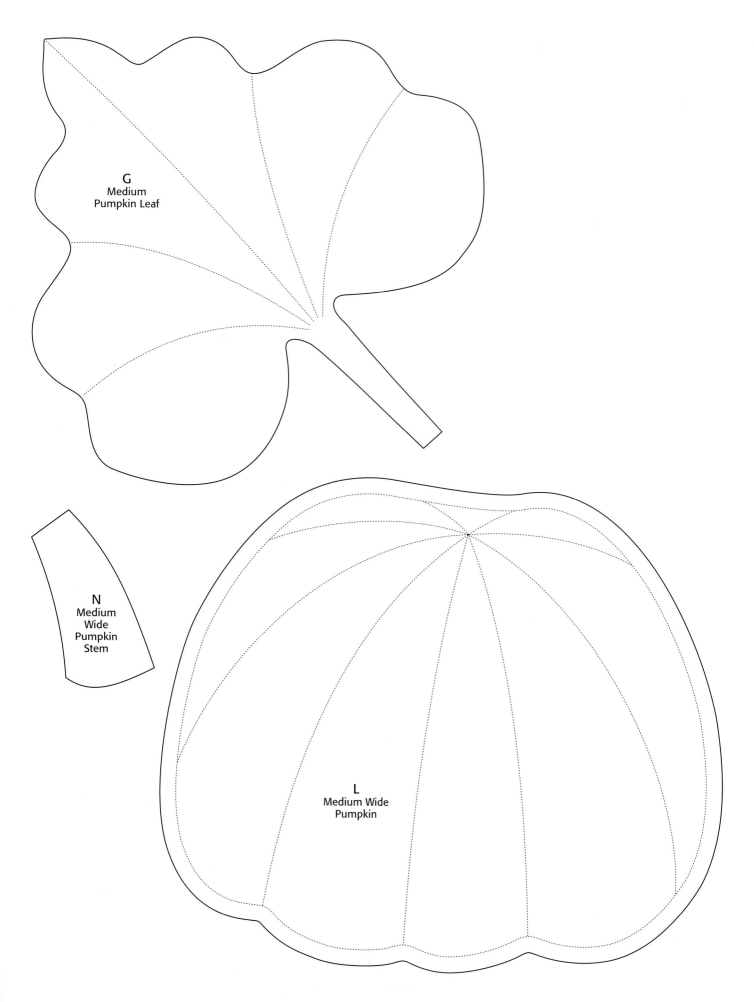

G
Medium
Pumpkin Leaf

N
Medium
Wide
Pumpkin
Stem

L
Medium Wide
Pumpkin

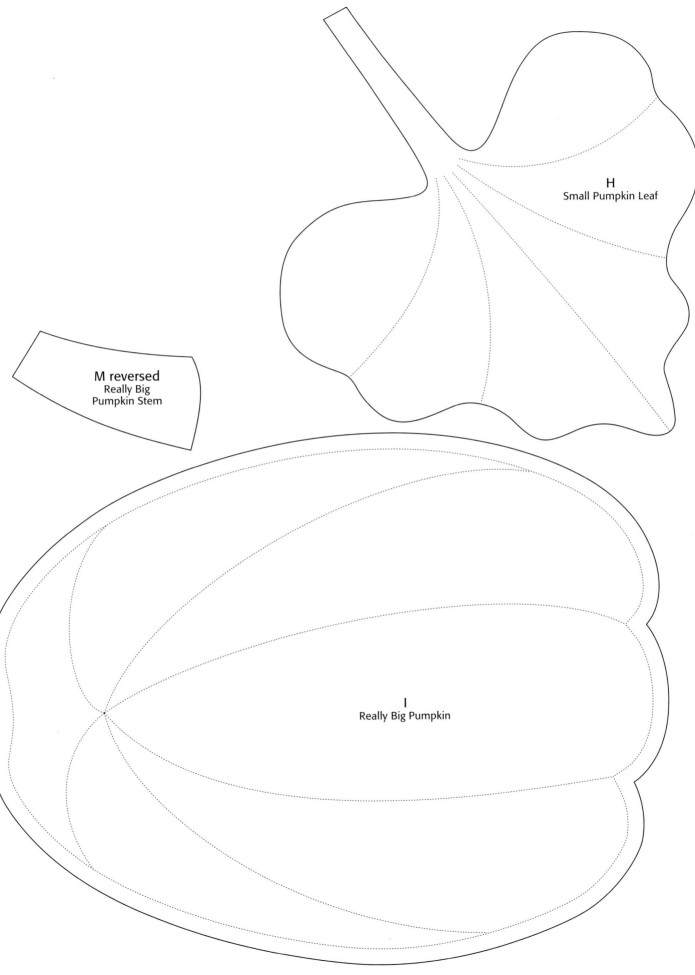

H
Small Pumpkin Leaf

M reversed
Really Big
Pumpkin Stem

I
Really Big Pumpkin

Filbert Tree

We have planted hundreds of filbert trees on our Whidbey Island farm. Although they vary in variety and age, the basic shape remains the same. This is my autumn interpretation of this wonderfully formed tree, complete with a filbert-print border. The treetop is embellished with buttons, charms, and floss tails, and the fence sections come to life with yo-yo sunflowers and fusible birdhouse and flower motifs.

You may want to make this into your own special tree, such as an apple tree with spring blossoms or the fall version covered with mature fruit, and border the quilt with a coordinating theme print. Whatever the tree or season, you are going to love making this quilt!

FINISHED QUILT SIZE: 28½" x 34"

Materials

Yardage is based on 42"-wide fabric.

- ½ yard *total* of assorted tan fabrics and cream fabrics for treetop background
- ¼ yard *total* of assorted brown fabrics for trunk and branches
- ¼ yard of tan fabric for center section background and first background row of fence section
- ¼ yard *total* of assorted green, rust, gold, and orange fabrics for leaves
- ¼ yard of dark purple fabric for fence
- ¼ yard *total* of assorted yellow fabrics for sunflowers
- ⅛ yard *total* of 2 assorted tan fabrics and/or cream fabrics for second and third background rows of fence section
- ⅛ yard *total* of assorted green fabrics for sunflower stems and leaves
- ⅝ yard of coordinating theme print for border
- 1 yard of fabric for backing
- ½ yard of fabric for binding
- Craft-size batting (36" x 46")
- Assortment of buttons and charms
- Embroidery floss in an assortment of colors to match leaf fabrics
- Fusible motifs: one 1½" x 2" birdhouse, one ½" ladybug, and four ⅝"-diameter sunflowers
- 3 brown buttons for centers of yo-yo sunflowers
- Template plastic
- Hand-sewing needles: Sharp and embroidery
- ⅛ yard of fusible transfer web

DESIGN DETAIL

Visually, this quilt can be broken down into three sections: the treetop section, the center section, and the fence section. To create the illusion of light filtering through the treetop, use a variety of tan and cream background fabrics in the treetop section. The center section uses just one background fabric. This same fabric is used for the first row of the fence section and is also incorporated into the treetop section. Using the same fabric helps the sections blend together better, although you could certainly use a variety of fabrics if that is more to your liking. The fence section also uses two additional cream and/or tan background fabrics in addition to the fabric used in the center section.

Cutting

From the tan fabrics and cream fabrics for treetop background, cut a *total* of:

- 1 strip, 2" x 21½"
- 1 strip, 1½" x 9½"
- 1 strip, 1½" x 8½"
- 1 strip, 1½" x 7½"
- 2 strips, 1½" x 6½"
- 3 strips, 1½" x 5½"
- 5 strips, 1½" x 4½"
- 1 strip, 1½" x 3½"
- 33 rectangles, 1½" x 2½"
- 39 squares, 1½" x 1½"

Continued on page 68

From the assorted green, rust, gold, and orange fabrics, cut a *total* of:

- 35 rectangles, 1½" x 2½"
- 41 squares, 1½" x 1½"

From the assorted brown fabrics, cut a *total* of:

- 1 strip, 2½" x 13½"
- 3 rectangles, 1½" x 2½"
- 11 squares, 1½" x 1½"

From the tan fabric for center section background and first background row of fence section, cut:

- 1 strip, 4½" x 11½"
- 1 rectangle, 4½" x 8½"
- 1 strip, 2" x 20"
- 1 strip, 1½" x 15"; crosscut the strip to make 9 squares, 1½" x 1½"

From the 2 assorted tan fabrics and/or cream fabrics for second and third background rows of fence section, cut a *total* of:

- 1 strip, 1¾" x 20"
- 1 strip, 1¼" x 20"

From the dark purple fabric, cut:

- 2 strips, 1½" x 42"; crosscut the strips to make 9 strips, 1½" x 5½"
- 1 strip, 1¼" x 42"; crosscut the strip to make 2 strips, 1¼" x 20"

From the assorted green fabrics for sunflower stems and leaves, cut:

- 1 strip, 1" x 18"

From the coordinating theme print, cut:

- 4 strips, 4½" x 42"

From the binding fabric, cut:

- 4 strips, 3" x 42"

Assembling the Wall Hanging Top

1. Assemble the treetop background, tree, and leaf pieces together into three sections as shown. Stitch the pieces in each row of each section together. Press the seams toward the tree and leaf sections. Stitch the rows of each section together. Press the seams toward the bottom of the quilt. Set the sections aside.

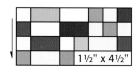

2. To make the fence-rail sections, stitch the 20"-long background and fence strips together along the long edges in the order shown to make a strip set. Press the seams toward the fence strips.

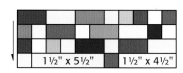

3. From the strip set, cut one segment 2½" wide and eight segments 1½" wide.

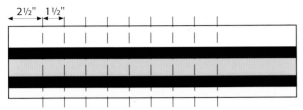

Cut 1 segment 2½" wide and 8 segments 1½" wide.

4. To make the fence pickets, using the marking tool of your choice, draw a diagonal line on the wrong side of the nine 1½" fence background squares.

5. With right sides together and raw edges aligned, place a marked background square on one end of each dark purple 1½" x 5½" fence strip. Stitch directly on the diagonal line. Cut away the excess fabric, leaving a ¼" seam allowance. Press the seams toward the fence strip. Make nine.

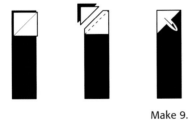

Make 9.

> ## TIP
> The more variety in the top and background fabric, and the more buttons, charms, and floss, the better!

6. Stitch the fence pickets and fence-rail segments into two sections as shown. Press the seams toward the pickets.

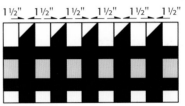

Left Section

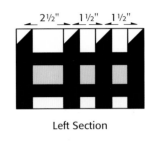

Right Section

7. Stitch the treetop lower right and left sections, the center section background pieces, and the right and left fence sections together as shown. Press the seams toward the center sections.

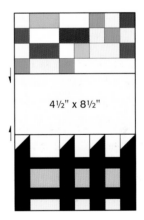

4½" x 8½"

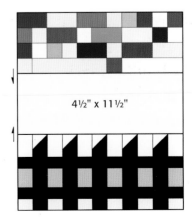

4½" x 11½"

8. Sew the brown 2½" x 13½" strip between the left and right sections from step 7. Press the seams toward the brown strip.

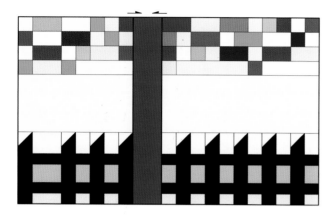

9. Stitch the treetop top section to the upper edges of the pieced section from step 8. Press the seam toward the treetop lower sections.

10. Refer to "Making Templates" on page 9 to trace patterns A and B on page 72 onto template plastic. Using the templates, trace two of A and one of B onto the wrong side of the assorted yellow fabrics. Cut out the circles.

11. Thread the Sharp needle with yellow all-purpose thread and knot the ends together. Finger-press under the edges of each circle ⅛". Sew a running stitch close to the folded edge of each circle. When you have stitched completely around the circle, pull up the thread tightly to gather the circle edge; knot the threads to secure them. The yo-yo gathered side is the right side. Set aside the yo-yos. They will be attached after the borders are added.

12. For the sunflower stems, stitch the green 1" x 18" strip in half lengthwise, wrong sides together, using a ⅛" seam allowance. Press the seam open while you press the strip flat. Trim the seam allowance if necessary. From the strip, cut one segment 5" wide, one segment 5½" wide, and one segment 6" wide.

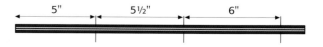

13. Pin the stem segments in place as shown, making sure the ends extend beyond the bottom edge of the quilt top. Using matching thread, stitch along both sides of each stem segment.

Finishing the Wall Hanging

Refer to "Quilt Finishing" on pages 73–78.

1. Stitch the 4½"-wide coordinating-theme-print strips to the top and bottom edges of the quilt top and then to the sides. Press the seams toward the borders.

2. Referring to "Fusible-Web Appliqué" on page 13 and using the patterns on page 72, trace four of pattern C and five of pattern C reversed onto the paper side of the fusible web. Cut around the shapes. Fuse each appliqué shape to the wrong side of a green fabric piece. Cut out the appliqués on the drawn lines and remove the paper backing.

3. Arrange the leaves on the stems as shown; fuse in place. Using a satin stitch, stitch around the edges of each leaf.

4. Center a fabric yo-yo over the top end of each sunflower stem. Stitch a button to the center of each yo-yo, stitching through all the layers to secure the yo-yo.

5. Follow the manufacturer's instructions to fuse the motifs to the fence section, referring to the photo on page 66 for placement.

6. Layer the quilt top with batting and backing; baste.

7. Quilt as desired.

8. Arrange the buttons and charms on the tree-top leaf pieces as desired. Thread the embroidery needle with six strands of embroidery floss in the desired color. Stitch each button and charm to the quilt top, leaving a thread tail at the beginning and end. Tie the tails in a knot and trim the ends to a uniform length. In the same manner, add thread tails to any of the remaining leaf pieces that do not have a button or charm.

9. Bind the edges of the quilt.

10. Add a hanging sleeve and label if desired.

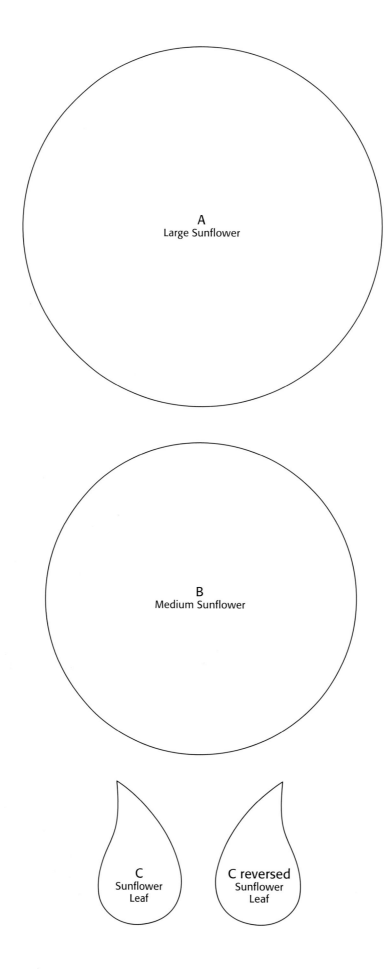

A
Large Sunflower

B
Medium Sunflower

C
Sunflower
Leaf

C reversed
Sunflower
Leaf

Quilt Finishing

Adding Borders

THE QUILTS IN this book all feature borders with straight-cut corners. Cut the border strips across the width of the fabric unless otherwise instructed. All of the strips are cut to avoid piecing. The strips will be cut longer than needed and then trimmed to size.

To stitch the borders to the quilt top, follow these instructions:

1. Measure the width of the quilt top through the horizontal center. Trim two border strips to this measurement. Mark the center of the border strips and the quilt-top top and bottom edges.

2. With right sides together, pin the border strips to the top and bottom edges of the quilt top, matching center marks and ends. Stitch the borders in place, easing in any excess fabric as needed. Press the seams toward the border strips.

3. Measure the length of the quilt top through the vertical center, including the top and bottom borders. Cut two border strips to this measurement, piecing and trimming strips as necessary to achieve the required length. Mark the center of the border strips and quilt-top side edges.

4. With right sides together, pin the border strips to the sides of the quilt top, matching center marks and ends. Stitch the borders in place, easing in any excess fabric as needed. Press the seams toward the border strips.

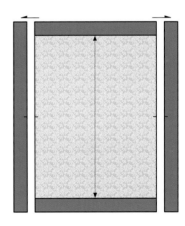

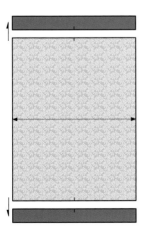

TIP

If the quilt top and border strips are not exactly the same length, layer the pieces so the longer piece is on the bottom when stitching. The sewing machine's feed dogs will help ease in the extra length.

Choosing Batting

There are many different types of batting, and new ones are always being introduced, so how do you decide which one to use? The first thing you need to do is to determine whether you will be hand or machine quilting the project. Some battings are more suitable for hand quilting because they are easier to needle, while others handle better when machine quilting. Because of the trims and embellishments on these quilts, they were all machine quilted. For machine quilting, I find that a cotton batting works best. My batting of choice is Quilters Dream Cotton, which is available in four weights and six sizes.

The project's end use should also be a factor when you select a batting. Are you using the batting as a wall hanging, a bed quilt, or a garment? Battings that drape well are more preferable for bed quilts and garments, while a stiffer batting is good for wall hangings. Wall hangings like "Cosmic Pumpkins" require a stiffer batting to support the weight of the embellishments.

Consider, also, how the project will be cleaned. An easy-care batting such as polyester is a good choice for bed quilts and garments that may be washed frequently.

You may have already developed your own batting preferences, but if not, hand and machine quilt a few samples, using a variety of battings sandwiched between a top and bottom fabric, to help you determine which batting handles best and gives you the desired look and feel.

Layering and Basting

Layering the quilt top, batting, and backing and temporarily joining the layers together with basting must be done before the project is quilted. It is critical that the layers be joined correctly in this step; any wrinkles or folds will be emphasized when you quilt the project. To help make the process easier and more accurate, assemble the layers on a work surface large enough to accommodate the entire project.

1. Press the quilt top from the back—this is the last opportunity to set the seams in the correct direction. Once your seams are set, press from the front. Use spray starch or sizing if desired.

2. Cut the backing and batting about 4" larger than the quilt top so you have about 2" extra on all sides.

3. Press the backing fabric. Use spray starch or sizing if desired.

4. Lay the backing, right side down, on a clean, flat surface. Secure it with masking tape in several places along the edges. The fabric should be taut but not stretched. Lay the batting on the backing; secure with masking tape. Place the quilt top, right side up, over the batting; secure with masking tape.

5. Beginning in the center of the quilt top and working toward the center of the quilt's outer top edge, hand baste the layers together. Return to the center, basting to the quilt's outer bottom edge. Continue basting vertically, spacing the rows about 4" apart. Repeat the process to baste the vertical rows and then the two diagonal rows. Complete the basting process by basting around the entire outer edge. I prefer hand basting with thread to pin basting because it allows me to

machine quilt without stopping to remove pins.

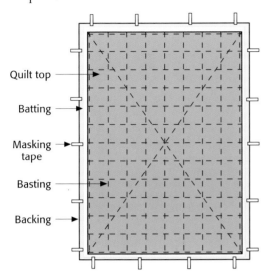

Quilt top

Batting

Masking tape

Basting

Backing

6. After basting the quilt, remove the tape. You are now ready to quilt!

Quilting

Machine quilting is recommended for the quilts in this book. Many of the quilts are heavily layered as well as richly embellished, and hand quilting would be difficult.

Choose a quilting design and thread that will complement your quilt but not overwhelm the embellishments. The embellishments are the focus of these projects, and you do not want the quilting to detract from them.

Squaring Up a Quilt

When you have completed the quilting, you will need to square up your quilt. This means cutting off the excess backing and batting, as well as cleaning up any threads or uneven sections of border.

Align a ruler with the seam of the outer border and measure to the edge of the quilt in a number of places. Use the narrowest measurement as a guide for positioning your ruler and trimming the excess all around the quilt.

Next, fold the quilt in half; then fold it again in the other direction. Does your quilt have square corners and edges that are equal in length? If not, this is your last chance to correct them. Use a large square ruler to square up the corners.

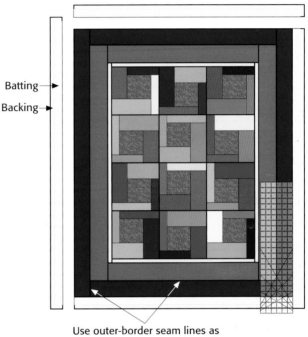

Batting

Backing

Use outer-border seam lines as a guide for squaring up the quilt.

Use a basting or serpentine stitch around the edge to stabilize the quilt—do not use a zigzag stitch. Once you have squared up your quilt top, you are ready for the finishing touches: the binding, hanging sleeve, and label.

Binding

The construction of your binding is very important. Working as a judge in quilt competitions has made this abundantly clear to me. Participants do not always take care with their bindings, and a poorly made binding can make an otherwise lovely quilt look sloppy. The following binding method combines the best of detail, strength, and beauty.

1. Cut enough 3"-wide binding strips to equal the perimeter of the quilt plus 15" for seams

and corners. Cut the strips across the width of the fabric unless otherwise indicated. I cut strips on the bias only if I want to take advantage of a diagonal print or if I need to fit the binding around rounded corners.

2. Join the strips at right angles as shown to make one long continuous strip. Trim the seam allowances to ¼" and press the seams open.

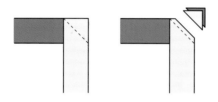

3. Press the binding in half lengthwise, wrong sides together.

Fold line

4. With raw edges even, lay the binding on the quilt top, 8" from the upper left-hand corner. Lay out the binding to the first corner. If a seam on the binding falls at the corner, adjust the binding accordingly. Begin stitching 6" from the end of the binding (14" from the corner), using a ½"-wide seam allowance.

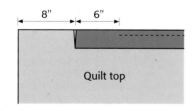
Quilt top

5. Stitch about 2", stop, and cut the threads. Remove the quilt from the machine and fold the binding to the back; it should barely cover the stitching line you just made. If the binding overlaps the stitching line too much, stitch again, just outside the first stitching line. If the binding doesn't cover the original stitching, stitch just inside the original stitching. Remove the extra stitches before you proceed.

6. Using the stitching position you determined in step 5, stitch to within ½" of the first corner. Stop, backstitch, cut the thread, and remove the quilt from the machine.

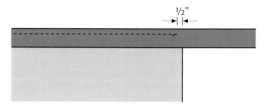
½"

7. Fold the binding up to create a 45° angle. Holding the folded edge in place, fold the binding down, having the new fold even with the top edge of the quilt and the raw edge aligned with the side of the quilt. Beginning ½" from the edge, stitch the binding to the quilt, stopping ½" from the next corner. Repeat the folding and stitching process for the remaining corners. Stop stitching about 3" after you turn the last corner.

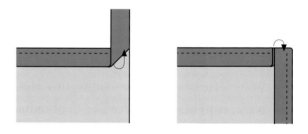

8. After turning the last corner, stitch about 3"; backstitch, and remove the quilt from the machine. Cut the ending tail of the binding so it overlaps the beginning tail of the binding by 3".

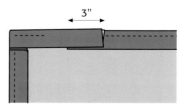
3"

9. Lay the quilt so the top is right side up. Unfold the unstitched ends of the binding tails. Place the tail ends right sides together at right angles, and pin. Draw a line from the upper left-hand corner to the lower right-hand corner of the binding. Stitch along this line.

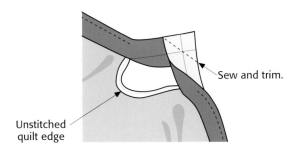

Sew and trim.

Unstitched quilt edge

10. Check to make sure the binding is the correct length for covering the unbound edge of the quilt. Carefully trim the seam allowance to ¼". Press the seam open. Re-press the binding in half. Finish stitching the binding to the quilt.

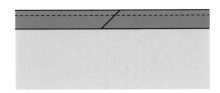

11. Fold the binding to the back of the quilt and pin it in place. I pin approximately 12" at a time. Hand stitch the binding to the quilt back, matching the thread to the binding and carefully mitering the corners. Hand stitch down each side of the mitered corners.

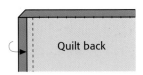

Quilt back

Adding a Hanging Sleeve

If you want to display your quilt on a wall, you need to add a sleeve to protect your work of art from undue strain.

1. Cut an 8½"-wide strip of backing fabric across the width of the fabric (if the quilt is wider than 40", cut two strips and stitch them together end to end). Cut the strip 1" shorter than the width of your quilt. Press the short ends under ¼" and stitch in place.

2. Fold the sleeve in half lengthwise, right sides together. Stitch along the long raw edges. Press the piece, creating a crease in the folded edge. Turn the sleeve to the right side. With the seam positioned at the center of the piece, press the sleeve again, creasing the opposite folded edge.

3. Mark the center of the quilt-top edge and the center of the long, folded edges of the sleeve. With the center marks aligned, pin the sleeve to the quilt back, placing one folded edge of the sleeve next to the binding. Blindstitch the folded edge in place.

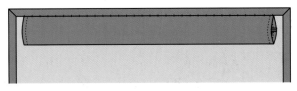

Blindstitch top of sleeve to quilt.

4. Push the bottom edge of the sleeve up just a bit to provide a little give so the hanging rod does not put strain on the quilt. Blindstitch the sleeve lower edge in place, being careful not to stitch through to the front of the quilt.

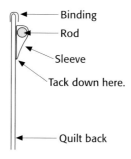

Binding
Rod
Sleeve
Tack down here.
Quilt back

Making a Label

Labels provide important information about you and your quilt. I make my labels about 4" x 7" so that I have plenty of room. Your labels should include at least the following:

- The name of the quilt
- Your full name
- Your business name, if applicable
- Your city, county, province and/or state, and country of residence
- The date
- Who the quilt was made for if you made it for a specific person, or why you made the quilt if you made it for a particular event

You may also wish to add the following information to the label:

- What series the quilt belongs to, if applicable
- A quilting teacher's name, if applicable
- A story connected with the piece, especially a heartfelt one

There are many ways to make a label. If your sewing machine has a lettering system, use it. If you own or have access to an embroidery machine, use it. Embroidery machines offer wonderful opportunities for embellishing your label. You may even want to create your own logo.

Other label-making methods include drawing and writing with permanent fabric markers and using photo-transfer techniques. If you use permanent markers, be sure to back the label with freezer paper, stabilizer, or interfacing while you letter it.

You may also want to include embroidered patches, decals, buttons, ribbons, or lace. Simply stitch them to the label to make it as unique as you are. I also like to include leftover blocks to link the quilt top to the back.

When is the correct time to attach your label? You can sew it to the lower right corner of the quilt back before it is basted or quilted. Or, you can attach your label after the quilting is complete.

Resources

The following companies, with the exception of Pacific Fabrics & Crafts and Island Fabrics Etc., are distributors and do not sell directly to consumers. Check your local quilt and fabric stores for products from these companies. If the products are not available locally, contact the company for a mail-order source.

Batting
Quilters Dream Batting
589 Central Dr.
Virginia Beach, VA 23454
888-268-8664
www.quiltersdreambatting.com

Threads, stabilizers, temporary spray adhesive, and other machine-embroidery supplies and books
Sulky of America
www.sulky.com

Threads
Robison-Anton Textiles
175 Bergen Blvd.
Fairview, NJ 07022-1619
800-932-0250
www.robison-anton.com

American & Efird, Inc.
Exclusive U.S. importer of Mettler threads
PO Box 507
Mount Holly, NC 28120
800-847-3235
www.amefird.com
consumer.homepage@amefird.com

Fusible web
Therm O Web
770 Glenn Ave.
Wheeling, IL 60090
800-323-0799
www.thermoweb.com

Fabrics, trims, threads, notions, books, and crafting supplies
Pacific Fabrics & Crafts
2230 4th Ave. S
Seattle, WA 98134
206-628-2222
www.pacificfabrics.com

Island Fabrics Etc.
1609 E. Main St.
PO Box 697
Freeland, WA 98249
360-331-4435
www.islandfabrics.com

Sewing machines and accessories, sewing notions, software, and Sylvia sewing furniture
Husqvarna Viking
31000 Viking Pkwy.
Westlake, OH 44145-8012
800-358-0001

Viking Distributing Co., Inc.
685 Market St.
Medford, OR 97504
800-428-2804

Quilt and needle-art supplies
Quilter's Resource
PO Box 148850
Chicago, IL 60614
773-278-5695
www.quiltersresource.com

About the Author

M'Liss Rae Hawley and Ch. Garden Court's Aurora Rae

M'LISS RAE HAWLEY began her lifelong textile adventure at the age of four by embroidering a pillowcase with purple variegated floss. By the time she enrolled in a high-school sewing class, she had been working with needle and thread for so long that the nuns discovered quite soon that she had more experience than they did! M'Liss studied at the University of Washington in the textiles and clothing department, and then continued her studies in Central Washington University's graduate program.

This is M'Liss's fourth book with Martingale & Company. Her books *Fat Quarter Quilts* and *More Fat Quarter Quilts* are both bestsellers. Her most recent accomplishments include designing embroidery motifs for Husqvarna Viking embroidery cards. The designs coordinate with her fabric lines, manufactured by Clothworks. M'Liss and her dachshund Gorgeous George were featured in Bernina of America's Portrait of the Artist ad campaign. Her work has been featured in many national quilting magazines, and she is a regular contributor to *McCall's Quilting, McCall's Quick Quilts,* and *Quilt Magazine.* M'Liss has also appeared on PBS cooking and quilting shows.

M'Liss lives on a small filbert farm on Whidbey Island, Washington, with her husband, four dachshunds, three cats, and an assortment of drop-ins. Her husband, Michael, is the county sheriff and writes murder mysteries in his spare time. They have two children: Alexander, a corporal in the United States Marine Corps, and Adrienne, a college student.